Queen Esther
and the Ring of Power

Colombia para Cristo video introduction

Watch the *La Montaña* trailer, a film based on a true Stendal event

Queen Esther
and the Ring of Power

Prophetic Voice
for the End Times

Russell M. Stendal

Visit Russell's website: www.cpcsociety.ca
Queen Esther – Russell M. Stendal
Copyright © 2015
First edition published 2015

All rights reserved. No part of this book may be reproduced, stored in a retrieval system, or transmitted in any form or by any means – electronic, mechanical, photocopying, recording, or otherwise, without written permission from the publisher.

Scripture quotations are taken from the Jubilee Bible, copyright © 2000, 2001, 2010, 2013 by Life Sentence Publishing, Inc. Used by permission of Life Sentence Publishing, Inc., Abbotsford, Wisconsin. All rights reserved.

Cover Design: Amber Burger
Cover Photography: Ellerslie/Shutterstock
Editor: Ruth Zetek

Printed in the United States of America
By Aneko Press – *Our Readers Matter*™
www.anekopress.com
Aneko Press, Life Sentence Publishing, and our logos are trademarks of Life Sentence Publishing, Inc.
203 E. Birch Street
P.O. Box 652
Abbotsford, WI 54405
RELIGION / Biblical Biography / Old Testament
Paperback ISBN: 978-1-62245-267-5
Ebook ISBN: 978-1-62245-268-2
10 9 8 7 6 5 4 3 2 1
Available wherever books are sold.
Share this book on Facebook:

Contents

Introduction IX

Ch. 1: The Royal Feast 1

Ch. 2: The Search for a New Queen 17

Ch. 3: Haman's Hatred 31

Ch. 4: Esther Risks Everything 53

Ch. 5: Reward for Mordecai 67

Ch. 6: Esther's Plea 91

Ch. 7: Our Defense 115

Ch. 8: Destruction and Victory 127

Ch. 9: The End of Haman's Sons 135

Conclusion 151

About the Author 169

Introduction

Upon occasion, I have been able to identify with Mordecai and Esther in sensing the towering hatred that Haman had towards all the people of God. Over five hundred of my close friends and acquaintances have been killed here in Colombia. More pastors have been tortured or killed in Colombia over the past twenty years than in any other country upon the face of the earth. According to the United Nations, we now have more than six million displaced persons, most of them Christians (this is surpassed only by Syria). In the great violence between 1948 and 1958, a very large percentage of the evangelical Christians in Colombia were killed in an all-out attempt to exterminate the true people of God.

I have been taken hostage five times by guerrillas, captured three times by rogue paramilitary forces, and jailed twice by the government. Numerous attempts have been made upon my life. Yet my worst enemies are not the armed actors of the Colombian war (many of whom have come to the Lord), but rather the religious factions who fear that our literature and radio broadcasts will cause the people to escape from their heavy hand and emancipate them into the liberty of the Holy Spirit. Multiplied thousands are finding freedom as one of the greatest revivals in history has been ignited in this land and has been steadily building since 1932. Since this is taking place in the midst of severe persecution but is not in the limelight, it has been difficult for anyone to contaminate it.

A few weeks ago a missionary associate of ours named Pabel was brutally murdered. He was stalked for six months and then tied to a tree and strangled by the weight of the bag of Bibles that he always carried with him on his motorcycle. In early December of 2014, another one of my friends was imprisoned for trumped-up charges of rebellion and for being my guide into rebel areas of the high country (páramo). When our lawyer requested the audio of the court hearing, a mistake was made, and she was given a copy of a secret court hearing against me that indicated there was a warrant out for my arrest. It was similar to when Mordecai sent a copy of the edict against the Jews to Queen Esther.

I had just finished checking the new modern-English edition that we did of *The Pilgrim's Progress* (by Aneko Press), where we printed out the Scripture references from the *Jubilee Bible* into the text and retained the original art and poetry. So I remembered the story of John Bunyan. He wrote most of *The Pilgrim's Progress* in prison, and then one day he was released. Happily, he continued his ministry of traveling and preaching.

One of his friends told him that he should finish his book because he felt that undoubtedly it would prove to be much more important than itinerant ministry. John Bunyan put off finishing the book and continued to preach. Soon he was arrested again and remained in prison until the book was finished. You know the rest of the story. *The Pilgrim's Progress* has been second only to the Scriptures in distribution and impact among the English-speaking world. In fact, our society today would be different if not for that book.

So I remembered three manuscripts that I had on the back burner. I had also promised the Lord to translate at least one hundred messages out of the more than one thousand effective

Spanish messages that I have preached on the radio in the Colombian war zone, so they might be published in English. The police stopped me as I headed out of town to a remote location where I would continue my writing. They examined my ID, and one of them asked the others if they should run my name through their computer system and check my record. I winced, knowing that if they did that I could be arrested, and in Colombia, there is no bail. People can spend years in prison before getting a trial. The policeman looked into my eyes and said to his partners, "No need to look this one up in the system; he looks like an honest guy!"

I holed up in a secure location provided by the Lord in the midst of several lakes (seemed like the garden of Eden) and finished my three manuscripts in record time: this one on Esther, another on Peter, and one on the first half of the book of Revelation. This brings me up to eighty-three messages translated into English that will be published. (I was brought up on John Wesley's one hundred standard sermons that helped spark the Great Awakening.)

Friends in high places soon rallied to my aid, but I felt like Martin Luther, confined to the castle of his friend, as the Colombian judicial system took on a life of its own. Even my phones were being wiretapped, and my email accounts intercepted. It was a moment of truth, and I found out how many real friends I have, as I remembered the story of how William Tyndale was betrayed to his death by someone he thought he could trust.

From my place of hiding, I found ways to help the widow and the two orphans of my ministry associate who had been killed. I was also able to implement a legal strategy for the defense of my jailed friend and myself, while running dozens of controversial radio stations and deploying tens of thousands of parachutes with gospel literature into extremely dangerous remote areas.

A few weeks before, on October 19, I had been taken hostage for several days by a rogue paramilitary unit that was apparently trying to determine if they could kill my radio technicians and me and throw a monkey wrench into the Colombian peace process. Miraculously, the Lord sent a Colombian Special Forces unit under the command of an honest young corporal who extricated us from that precarious situation.

One of our best and most influential radio stations is run by two brothers. One brother was put in jail by the government (and is still there), and the other is on a hit list from the guerrillas (but the assassin sent to kill him was captured and the truth became known). In and through it all, we have been able to keep what is possibly our most powerful and effective station on the air and to continue to minister deep inside rebel territory.

Months before, I had booked tickets to travel to a missions convention in Canada where I needed to attend our annual board meeting, and then travel to the US and meet with leaders of another key ministry. My flight was due to leave at 1:00 a.m. and the phone rang at 10:00 p.m. It was a top general. He said that as far as he knew, the charges against me had evaporated and I would be able to pass through immigration without being arrested. Nothing could be found against me in the legal system, but he said he was still investigating to find out who would have done such a thing as to file false secret charges against me in the first place. A prime suspect is a religious organization cloaked in secrecy that is also suspected of being behind the murder of Pabel.

I had just enough time to catch the flight, and my trip went like clockwork.

As I have identified with Mordecai and Esther, I see the book of Daniel setting the context for the book of Esther. Darius the

Mede in the book of Daniel is likely the same person as King Ahasuerus in the book of Esther (see page 10 in *The Correction Factor*[1] – a commentary on the book of Zechariah). If this is the case, then the book of Esther is the sequel to the book of Daniel and takes place concurrently with the books of Ezra, Zechariah, and Haggai, with the book of Nehemiah being the sequel to the book of Esther.

If we compare Daniel to the prophet Elijah, Mordecai would be similar to Elisha, who received a double portion of the spirit of Elijah. Elisha mentored a "school of the prophets," and one of Elisha's young prophets anointed Jehu and set the stage for the death of two wicked kings and Jezebel. Under Elijah, the prophets of Baal were killed (1 Kings 18:40), and under Elisha, all the followers of Baal were destroyed (2 Kings 10:20-28).

Mordecai raised Esther. Esther won the kingdom, destroyed Haman, the archenemy of the people of God, and even managed to kill all of his sons and followers, setting the stage for a golden age of restoration of Israel under the government of God, which was only a type and shadow of things to come.

A close study of the Great Awakening that began more than 275 years ago will show that many spontaneous messages were preached under the anointing of the Holy Spirit (a good place to start is the journal of John Wesley). Seemingly obscure Old Testament passages were treated as true-life parables and yet with vivid interpretation by the Holy Spirit involving allegory. For example, see the *Massachusetts Missionary Magazine* for the year 1806, published in Boston and printed by E. Lincoln, Water-Street, regarding the life of William Tennent (a contemporary ministry associate of George Whitefield) and of many other people used by God in the Great Awakening. The account

---

1 Russell M. Stendal, *The Correction Factor: Zechariah: A Key to Unlock the Book of Revelation* (Aneko Press, 2014), 10.

of two most-extraordinary, spontaneous messages is recorded on pages 48 to 50 that took place about 1744.

Hundreds of preachers were able to open their Bibles anywhere in the Scriptures at the drop of a hat, and their messages would flow and bring their audiences under great conviction. Most of the time, they were unable to finish due to the loud cries of those who were repenting, in a day when there were very large crowds and no loudspeakers. Unfortunately, due to the lack of recording devices, only the prepared messages that were written out in advance have survived, hundreds of which, however, are readily accessible on Internet.

I see the present revival in Colombia (from which the spontaneous messages contained in this volume flow) as a continuation of what God has been doing over the centuries with the Reformation and the Great Awakening. A major distraction over the past century has diminished the force and flow of revival in North America. This happens when theologians (and the reference materials they produce) derive the meaning of the key words used in Scripture by giving priority to contemporary pagan meanings instead of looking at God's introduction, development, and final usage of these words and key concepts throughout the Bible, starting with the narrative of the Hebrew Old Testament, then into the prophets, and then the transition into the Greek of the New Testament.

The Spanish edition of the *Jubilee Bible*, also known as *Reina Valera 2000* or *Version Antigua* (which I spent ten years translating), is designed to help the average person understand the simplicity of the Scriptures and is ideal for the leaders of the persecuted church who do not have a personal reference library. Millions of copies of this Spanish Bible are now in use. Just in the year 2000 alone, the first year that we put the audio version on Internet servers, there were more than two million free downloads. In this version, the same word is translated the same way throughout, doing away with the use of synonyms as much as possible. This allows the Bible to interpret itself. The key meanings of proper nouns and key terminology in this present work regarding the book of Esther are derived from this Spanish Bible, and the sources are listed on the flyleaf. (Please note that the Bible dictionary published in Spanish is much more extensive than the one published in the English *Jubilee Bible*).

Before I proceed, it is important to take note of the last thing that Jesus did before his ascension:

Luke 24

45 Then he opened their understanding that they might understand the scriptures.

Ask the Lord to open your understanding as you read the following pages. The value and interpretation given by the Holy Spirit to the story of Esther will undoubtedly require some readers to take a great leap of faith. If you proceed, I guarantee you will also experience a tremendous barrage of fiery darts from the Enemy that can only be quenched by the shield of faith (Ephesians 6:16). I do not expect you to be satisfied with my witness, however. It is my hope and prayer that you will be stirred and challenged until God opens your spiritual eyes and you receive your own witness.

The real fulfillment of the prophecies of Daniel and Esther are for us. We are entering the time of fullness and judgment. Some will enter in and others will be cut off. The fact that God has unsealed this message means that the time of fulfillment is upon us (Daniel 12:9). The realm of the Holy of Holies is before us.

Russell M. Stendal
February 18, 2015

P.S. A few hours after writing the above introduction, I received a communication from an Army officer suggesting that I see a police investigator at a nearby Bogota police station. It was a trap and they had a secret warrant out for my arrest. The next day, even before a court hearing, I was paraded in front of the news media and accused of rebellion against the government of Colombia (this would be like being accused of treason in the US). The story went around the world. Twenty poor *campesinos* were also jailed and the prosecutor claimed I was their leader.

We have spent several years distributing large quantities of Bibles, solar powered Galcom radios, and other Christian materials into remote rebel areas on horseback and by mule train. We were being accused of supplying the rebel guerrilla forces with anti-government paraphernalia, while what we actually distributed was Christian materials.

On the evening of February 19, after a five-hour court hearing in which I was accused for over three hours and allowed to speak for only ten minutes, the judge finally threw out the case of the prosecution and set me free unconditionally. The courtroom was packed and the hall of the courthouse was full of news media. Suddenly, the missionary work I had been doing in the shade was in the spotlight and the media was falling all over themselves trying to rectify the bad report that they had irresponsibly put out a few hours earlier, before the hearing. Over the next minutes, hours, days, and weeks, I was given many opportunities to tell the truth and to testify for the Lord over national and international media channels.

At first, after being arrested, I felt like Mordecai when he was sitting in sackcloth in front of the king's gate. All a sudden everything switched and it was more like being pranced around town on the king's horse and dressed in the king's clothes with the media trumpeting all about the work I have been doing over the past several decades for the Lord.

Now we are in yet another stage in which the process in the judicial system continues against me while many friends in very high places are making special provision for my defense. This is somewhat parallel to when the decree that Haman sealed with the king's ring against the Jews could not be recalled but another decree allowing them to defend themselves was signed and sealed after the king took his ring back from Haman and gave it to Mordecai.

My case has rallied people of God while at the same time the enemies of the Gospel continue to work behind the scenes. All of this, however, is heading for a conclusion. I am convinced that the Lord is allowing me to live through this experience because the message contained in this book is timely and of utmost importance to the body of Christ in this most desperate and uncertain worldwide time of confusion. As the people of God, we need not be confused or dismayed. I hope that this prophecy of Queen Esther and the ring of power will be as encouraging to you as it has been to me.

Chapter 1

The Royal Feast

Esther 1

1 *Now it came to pass in the days of Ahasuerus (this is Ahasuerus who reigned from India even unto Ethiopia over one hundred and twenty-seven provinces)*

2 *That in those days, when the king Ahasuerus sat on the throne of his kingdom, which was in Shushan, the palace,*

3 *In the third year of his reign, he made a banquet unto all his princes and his slaves, having before him the power of Persia and Media, the governors and princes of the provinces,*

4 *to show them the riches of the glory of his kingdom and the honour of beauty of his greatness for many days, even one hundred and eighty days.*

5 *And when these days were expired, the king made a banquet unto all the people that were present in Shushan the palace, both unto great and small, for seven days, in the court of the garden of the king's palace.*

Ahasuerus" may have been a generic title for the king, such as "Pharaoh" in Egypt. The symbolic meaning of who the king really is starts out as an enigma and develops as the story moves forward. *Shushan*, meaning "lilies," is linked with the Holy Place of Solomon's temple, which is a symbol of the church and of the church age. The lily was prominent in the decoration of the Holy Place of the temple (1 Kings 7:19-22) and is used eighteen times in the Old Testament. The number eighteen also correlates with the Holy Place and the church in Old Testament typology. Psalm 18, written by David, gives a great prophetic description of what Jesus would later do with the Gentiles during the age of the church. David, as prophet, priest, and king, is a portrayal of Jesus Christ and of the body of Christ. Song of Solomon links the lily symbolically and prophetically to Jesus Christ and to his followers in the church (Song of Solomon 2:1, 16).

The time period is the third year of the kingdom, when the king held a banquet for 180 days for all the governors and princes, followed by a seven-day banquet for all the other people. This book is about Jews but is symbolic of the church and of how the church age will end. The Feast of Tabernacles is symbolic of the kingdom age that immediately follows the church age (which is ending).

In the types and signs and symbols of Scripture, Shushan, the palace (the open flower of the lily), is linked to the number eighteen (in this case, eighteen times ten), which represents an intermediate period (the church age) between the age of the law and the age of the kingdom. This is the story of how God plans to bring the body of Christ to maturity.

The Holy Place (Exodus 40:22-27) is the realm of the priesthood of all born-again believers, where the lampstand, made of sixty-six pieces of gold hammered together, portrays the sixty-six books of the Bible in the light of the anointing of the Holy Spirit. The table of the showbread signifies the body of Christ broken for us and the nourishment that every connecting bond supplies (Ephesians 4:16). The golden altar of incense represents the prayers that reach the throne of God in the realm of the Holy of Holies on the other side of the veil that separates the Holy Place from the direct presence of God.

The kingdom described here is of the *Medes* (meaning "center of the earth") and the *Persians* (meaning "eternal"). It is God's plan to unite once again the two realms. Due to the failure of our ancestors, Adam and Eve, there has been a divorce between heaven and earth. The book of Esther, with Esther representing the morning star, is the symbolic story of how God brings everything back together.

When the king began the feast, he said his purpose was

> 4 *to show them the riches of the glory of his kingdom and the honour of beauty of his greatness for many days, even one hundred and eighty days.*
>
> 5 *And when these days were expired, the king made a banquet unto all the people that were present in Shushan the palace, both unto great and small, for seven days, in the court of the garden of the king's palace.*

The *court of the garden* reminds us of the garden from which Adam and Eve were banished. This is the place of the direct presence of God. This place is linked to the coming age of the kingdom and is portrayed as the Holy of Holies in the temple. The veil dividing the two realms was embroidered with Cheribim and a flaming sword, which depicts the Genesis account of how Adam and Eve lost access to the garden and to the tree of life.

> 6 *There were white, green, and blue hangings, fastened with cords of fine linen and purple to silver rings and pillars of marble; the beds were of gold and silver, upon a pavement of porphyre and of marble and of alabaster and of blue.*

White represents holiness, which means being available for the exclusive use of the Lord. Green represents resurrection life; blue represents integrity (no hypocrisy); *fine linen* is the righteous acts of the saints; purple is royalty; and *silver rings* represent the power of redemption. The *pillars of marble* mean that this is supported by the very nature of God. *Beds . . . of gold and silver* mean the saints may rest upon the redemption accomplished by the very nature of God.

This is all set forth on a firm foundation of porphyry (an igneous rock that has had a change of nature), and of marble (pointing to the power and sufficiency of Christ), alabaster (remember the woman with the alabaster box who poured the precious perfume upon Jesus), and blue (integrity).

The root of the word *porphyry* means "purple" or "royalty." The original rock has red and white feldspar crystals embedded in a fine-grained dark red or purplish ground mass. The term is also used to describe a son, an heir to the throne who was born in the purple, and who was born after the parents ascended to the throne – a son born into nobility and freedom. All in the race of Adam are slaves to the flesh, the world, and the Devil; but Jesus Christ and those who are part of his body are free.

This is the case of all those truly born again into the life (and nature) of Jesus Christ when the Jerusalem of above, which is free, is the mother of us all (Galatians 4:26).

> 7 And they gave them drink in vessels of gold (the vessels being diverse one from another) and royal wine in abundance, according to the power of the king.

At God the King's party, all the vessels are gold, which represents his ministers and his nature. Each vessel is different. This feast is not according to the model of the previous feasts of Passover (law) and Pentecost (grace), which had limits (the anointing was limited or measured). This last feast has no limits.

There is *royal wine in abundance*: abundant life from God, abundant provision from God, and abundant provision for the kingdom. But there are two parties going on at the same time, and much of the church is at the wrong party.

In another parable, the invited guests did not come because some of them were inspecting new properties that they had purchased and others were trying out new yokes of oxen. They were caught up in their own kingdoms, attempting to do the work of God in the flesh (Luke 14:16-24).

> 8 *And the drink was according to this law: let no one constrain themselves; for so the king had appointed to all the officers of his house that they should do according to the will of each one.*

According to Scripture, the first feast, Passover (symbolically having to do with salvation), has one measure. The second feast, Pentecost (symbolically having to do with the infilling of the Holy Spirit), has three measures (because the Lord gives us more than what we need in Pentecost to see what we will do with the surplus). But the Feast of Tabernacles (symbolic of the coming fullness of the kingdom of God) is unlimited. Wine is a symbol of life (Psalm 104:15). However, we must be careful because it can represent our life or his life (Judges 9:13). Many have become intoxicated and obnoxious with the "wine" of their own lives. We are warned not to hurt the oil (the anointing of the Spirit) or the wine (of new life in Christ) because we could be disqualified from the fullness of the inheritance (Revelation 6:6).

> 9 *Likewise Vashti, the queen, made a banquet for the women in the royal house of King Ahasuerus.*

Queen Vashti did not arrive at the King's banquet of unlimited provision. She made her own banquet for the "women." Women are symbolic of congregations or churches. Many religious people continue to drink great and heady draughts of humanism.

> 10 *On the seventh day, when the heart of the king was merry with wine, he commanded Mehuman, Biztha, Harbona, Bigtha, Abagtha, Zethar, and Carcas, the seven eunuchs that served in the presence of Ahasuerus, the king,*
>
> 11 *to bring Vashti, the queen, before the king with the crown of the kingdom, to show the people and the princes her beauty, for she was fair to behold.*
>
> 12 *But Queen Vashti refused to come at the king's word by his eunuchs; therefore, the king was very wroth, and his anger burned within him.*

So a "Queen" is making her own banquet for all the other women (congregations) in the royal house of the King, even as they refuse to go to the King's banquet (which takes place in the realm of the Holy of Holies) and partake of the life (wine) of the King. It is time to celebrate the Feast of Tabernacles, but much of the church refuses to enter in.

Mehuman means "faithful."

Biztha means "loot."

Harbona means "ass herder."

Bigtha means "in the wine press."

Abagtha means "of the wine press."

Zethar means "star."

Carcas means "severe."

These eunuchs are in charge of the women. Today there are many congregations that are led by the equivalent, that are led by spiritual eunuchs. These eunuchs like to give orders, but they are incapable of begetting royal heirs; therefore, everything is sterile, yet still under the guise of a great banquet for women. Some of these names sound better than others and the king ordered all of them:

> 11 *to bring Vashti, the queen, before the king with the crown of the kingdom, to show the people and the princes her beauty, for she was fair to behold.*

The Lord has been waiting a long time for a bride (queen) without spot or wrinkle or any such thing. He desires to put his queen on display with the crown of the kingdom.

However, she who is presently the candidate for the crown has made her own banquet and will not respond to the orders of the King. She has been under the care of all these spiritual "eunuchs." This is the exact same situation that is going on now all over the world.

This parallels our present reality in that the beautiful "queen" is not fit to be put on display, nor does she desire in her heart to be so. She does not respond to the King even when he sends all the eunuchs.

So we come to the time when the king desires to put his queen on display, but she does not respond when summoned because she is doing her own thing. This is tragically the state of much of the church today.

People (and I am referring to both men and women) are operating gifts and talents from God for personal gain without tapping into the fullness of the power of God. There is a lot of church activity, but our problem is that the "queen" is dysfunctional. She is not humble, she is not submissive, and she does not even show up at the right party.

Jesus said that things would end in the following manner: Like a certain man, a king made a marriage feast for his son and sent invitations to the honored guests, but they would not come (Matthew 22:1-14). In this case, Vashti represents the honored guests who did not come. *Vashti* means "beautiful."

Queen Vashti's Punishment

> 13 *Then the king asked the wise men, who knew the times, (for so was the king's manner toward all that knew about the law and rights,*

The wise men know the times; they know what this represents. They also know about the law and about the rights of the king (and of the kingdom). The kingdom consists of the territory and of all the subjects who belong to the king.

The wise men of today know what time we are in; they know what God is about to show forth. They know it is the time for God to show forth the body of Christ as a bride waiting for her husband, without spot or wrinkle or any such thing; a bride who is not doing her own thing; a bride who is not exercising her own plans and ambitions.

> 14 *and the next to him was Carshena, Shethar, Admatha, Tarshish, Meres, Marsena, and Memucan, seven princes of Persia and Media, who saw the king's face, and who sat first in the kingdom;)*

Who are these seven individuals?

Carshena means "illustrious."

Shethar means "a star."

Admatha means "a testimony unto them."

It is clear that this trial is in front of a jury that is not only here on the earth, but also in heaven. In fact, it is in this feast that heaven and earth come back together. The Scripture speaks of a great cloud of witnesses (Hebrews 12:1). This is taking place in front of witnesses on earth and in heaven from Media (the realm of the earth) and from Persia (the eternal realm) in the "garden" of the palace. This equates to the realm of the Holy of Holies, which is behind the veil. This is the realm that Adam and Eve were banished from some six thousand years ago.

Tarshish is yellow beryl or yellow jasper. It means "strength" or "fortress." This is a precious stone that was on the pectoral of the breastplate of the high priest as the symbol of one of the tribes of Israel. It is also one of the nine precious stones that Satan was covered with before his fall (Ezekiel 28:13). The tarshish or beryl is located on the fourth row and in the first position (representing the tribe of Dan) over the heart of the high priest of the order of Aaron according to the Law of Moses (Exodus 28:20; Numbers 2). *Dan* means "judgment."

In the book of Revelation, under the ministry of Jesus, who is the High Priest under the order of *Melchisedec* (meaning "King of Righteousness"), the list and order of the tribes of Israel (the people of God) are revised. Two tribes, Ephraim and Dan, are eliminated and replaced with *Levi* (meaning "unity") and *Joseph* (meaning "let God add"). The tenth tribe, located in the position that had belonged to Dan, is now *Zebulun*, which means "dwelling in an intimate relationship." In the Feast of Tabernacles, Dan must be replaced by Zebulun (Revelation 7:4-12), and the position of *Ephraim*, meaning "double ash heap" (which can lead to double fruitfulness), is taken by *Simeon*, meaning "to hearken," or "to hear and obey."

Today, the people of God include both Jews and Gentiles (in unity among all those whom God has added), but there are still many tares (sons of the Evil One) planted in and among the wheat – among the church and among the Jews (1 Corinthians 12:13; Matthew 13:36-43). *People of God* is a scriptural term occurring in six verses. The first occurrence is in Judges 20:2, where the people of God include all who are gathered into his army from all the tribes of Israel. The last occurrence is in 1 Peter

2:10, which includes all the Gentiles who are being incorporated into the people of God after having obtained mercy. Scripture also uses the term *my people*, which is used in 220 verses from Genesis to Revelation and includes all of the redeemed.

Meres means "from above."

Marsena means "worthy."

Memucan means "dignified."

> 15 *What shall we do unto Queen Vashti according to law because she has not performed the decree of King Ahasuerus by the eunuchs?*

According to Scripture, the commandments of God are eternal (Psalm 119:98), and not one jot or one tittle of the law will pass away until all is fulfilled (Matthew 5:18). Many in the church, like Vashti, do not think that the law of God will judge them because they think they are under grace. But they fail to take into account that only those who are led by the Spirit of God are not under the law, and Vashti refused to enter the realm of the *garden of the king's palace*. There are requirements for entering into this realm: Anyone who does not repent or "afflict their soul" (turn their back on their own life) will be cut off from the people of God, and anyone who continues to do their own work shall be destroyed on the Day of Reconciliation (Leviticus 23:29) when it is time to enter the realm of the Holy of Holies. This is the realm of the Feast of Tabernacles.

The wheat and the tares can grow together in the feast of Pentecost (during the age of the church), but the tares will not be able to enter the Feast of Tabernacles because they will be cut off and destroyed (Matthew 13:38-43).

> 16 *And Memucan answered before the king and the princes, Vashti, the queen, has not only committed iniquity against the king, but also against all the*

princes and against all the people that are in all the provinces of King Ahasuerus.

17 For this deed of the queen shall be known abroad unto all the women so that they shall despise their husbands, saying, King Ahasuerus commanded Vashti, the queen, to be brought in before him, but she did not come.

18 And now the princesses of Persia and Media who have heard of the deed of the queen shall say this unto all the king's princes, and there shall be much contempt and wrath.

It is important to understand the meaning of the word *iniquity*. It means more than just "sin." To sin is to disobey the Word (or the law) of the Lord, but iniquity is when the sin is known to the sinner, and he or she chooses to hide it and continue in it.

Even though the Queen should have been at the king's banquet instead of making her own banquet, she could have been disoriented in her sin. However, when the seven eunuchs informed her of the king's order and she did not come, then it became iniquity.

The consequences of iniquity are more severe. The first use of this word in Scripture is when God confronted Cain after the death of his brother. When God asked about Abel, Cain replied, *I know not, Am I my brother's keeper?* when he had already killed him.

The Lord replied, *The voice of thy brother's blood cries unto me from the ground.* The Lord did not kill Cain; rather, he decreed that Cain should become a fugitive and a vagabond in the earth. Cain would never be at peace (Genesis 4:1-15). God was hoping that he would repent.

God's plan is to redeem the sinner, but when God dictated this sentence, Cain replied, *My iniquity is greater than I can bear*. This is the introduction of the word *iniquity* in Scripture (Genesis 4:13).

Vashti was not killed either. She was cut off, however, from being the queen.

It is possible for people to sin out of ignorance. They could be doing something in good faith and not know that they are going against God. However, it is not possible for them to commit iniquity and not know it. This is when they know about their sin, persist in it, and attempt to dissimulate it and hide it.

Iniquity will produce separation from God. Iniquity can go one more step and become rebellion. Rebellion is the same as witchcraft (1 Samuel 15:23). Rebellion is when someone knows the difference between God and Satan and openly sides with Satan.

Memucan asks what would happen if the queen insists on not complying with the will of the king. How would that affect all the provinces and all the peoples?

If the people of God, who are the closest to him, do not do what he says, then what about those who are not God's people? What about those who are still ignorant and are in need of a good example?

The greatest problem in the world right now (and facing all the true followers of the Lord) is not those who are out there apparently joined to the Enemy. It is not the world out there in darkness that cannot see the light.

The main problem in Jesus' day was not the publicans, the sinners, the prostitutes, or even the Romans. No, no, no. The main problem in Jesus' day was the scribes and Pharisees and priests who managed the Jewish religion. They had convinced themselves that they were fine. They were not only disobedient when Jesus came to give them light, but they rejected the light and tried to put it out! This is iniquity and rebellion.

The greatest problem in the world today is the banquet

prepared by "Vashti" for all the other "women" in the house of the King that is not the Feast of Tabernacles. And while the unlimited Feast of Tabernacles is served, they do not desire to come because they are unwilling to meet the basic requirements of the Day of Reconciliation; they are unwilling to repent and turn their backs on their own lives and "afflict their souls"; therefore, they are unable to cease from their own self-righteous works (Leviticus 23:29-31).

It has been possible up until now to enter the realm of the church, the realm of "Passover" (the plan of salvation), or even the realm of "Pentecost" (the infilling of the Holy Spirit) by simply agreeing with God, by agreeing to repent and believe. Entering the realm of the Feast of Tabernacles, however, is different. In order to enter this realm, there must be evidence of the fruit of the Spirit. There must be evidence that by the grace of God we have actually been brought to full repentance (turning from our own way) and to full dependence upon Jesus Christ. There must be evidence that he has truly cleansed our hearts, that he has brought forth godly character in us, that we enjoy pleasing him, and that we respond to his every command (Revelation 20:4-6).

The iniquity of Vashti became a bad example for all the other women, that is, for all the other congregations. If the queen does not obey the king, the entire kingdom will go off course.

> 19 *If it pleases the king, let there go forth a royal commandment from him, and let it be written among the laws of the Persians and the Medes, that it not be altered,*

Remember what happened when they wrote a law that said no one could pray except unto the king for a certain number of days? This is what set the stage for them to throw Daniel into the lion's den, because even the king could not alter the law. God, however, protected Daniel (Daniel 6).

Now the wise men are going to write another law that cannot be altered. This is the law:

> 19 *That Vashti come no more before King Ahasuerus, and let the king give her royal estate unto another that is better than she.*

Vashti, the queen, had been invited to come before all the governors, princes, and peoples of 127 provinces. She was to have the crown, the authority of the kingdom.

The Lord is preparing a people to manage a kingdom, and the requirement is for the people to have pure hearts. This queen had everything except a pure heart.

Adam and Eve had the crown; they received authority over all the earth, yet they turned their backs on God and placed their authority and crown into the hands of the deceiver. The real purpose of all these events and time periods is to straighten out the government and get it back under the direct command of the Lord. He has been preparing a people for this.

The eunuchs were ordered to bring Vashti before the king with the crown of the kingdom. She was not willing to come. She continued to do her own thing right in the same palace even when the king was calling her. We are in the same situation today. The Feast of Tabernacles is served, but the invited guests have not arrived and therefore cannot be crowned.

> 20 *And this sentence which the king shall make shall be heard throughout all his empire, although it is great, and all the wives shall give their husbands honour, from the greatest to the least.*
>
> 21 *And this word pleased the king and the princes, and the king did according to the word of Memucan;*

And if they make this law, remember that it cannot be changed or recalled.

Note that this is according to the word of *Memucan*, which means "dignified." This is a person who has the moral integrity, the transparency, the character to be giving this counsel to the king.

> 22 *for he sent letters into all the king's provinces,*
> *into every province according to the writing thereof,*
> *and to every people after their language, saying,*
> *That every man should bear rule in his own house*
> *and that it should be published according to the language of every people.*

In the New Testament, the chain of command mandated by God goes directly from Jesus to the man of each household, then to the wife, and finally to the children (Ephesians 5:22-25; 6:1-4; 1 Peter 3:1-7). Many clergy in the church today usurp control over the family unit and attempt to place themselves between the people and God. This limits freedom in Christ and enslaves the people.

In the English language, we are not able to catch all the details of the original language in which there were two possible words for *man*. The word for *man* used in verse 22 denotes a free or noble-born man as opposed to a slave.

In the beginning, Adam and Eve were free, but they delivered all of us into slavery. The only one after Adam and Eve who was born free was our Lord Jesus. Yet he was born of a woman who was part of a fallen, unclean creation.

Theologians have asked, If Mary was not born free and clean, how could she have a son who would be born free and clean?

Part of the answer is revealed when the angel visited Mary to announce the plan of God and she replied, *Behold, the handmaid [slave] of the Lord; be it unto me according to thy word* (Luke 1:30-38).

A slave of the Lord can be clean because the Lord is clean, and the slave belongs to the Lord.

When we are referred to as a congregation, male and female, as the people of God, this is always symbolized in Scripture as a woman. So, if we are part of the people of God (if we truly belong to the Lord), our true husband is the Lord. It is not possible to have the Feast of Tabernacles without restoring this order. Anyone (be it a group or an individual) who calls themselves by the name of the Lord and does not exclusively hear and obey the Lord is in the same situation as Vashti.

Unless this is corrected, there is no Feast of Tabernacles.

Let us pray:

Lord, we give you thanks for the opportunity that you have set before us. We ask that we might have wisdom and understanding of the time in which we live; that we might be able to see things from your perspective; that you may always lead us; that we may turn our backs on our own life so we may live your life. Amen.

Chapter 2

The Search for a New Queen

The previous chapter is the story of how Queen Vashti was invited to the banquet of the king but refused to go and continued making her own banquet instead. She lost the kingdom and set the stage for a new queen to be chosen.

Something similar is happening among the people of God today. The church (God's people are always represented as a woman in Scripture) has been invited by God to a feast of unlimited provision that God has prepared for this time. It is sad that many of the special invited guests have not responded to the invitation (Matthew 22:1-14). They are busily occupied with their own things. Now God is sending his invitation elsewhere because there is still room for more at his table at the Feast of Tabernacles.

Esther 2

1 After these things, when the wrath of King Ahasuerus was appeased, he remembered Vashti and what she had done and what was decreed against her.

2 Then the king's servants that ministered unto him said, Let there be fair young virgins sought for the king,

3 and let the king appoint officers in all the provinces of his kingdom that they may gather together

> all the fair young virgins unto Shushan, the palace, to the house of the women, unto the custody of Hegai, the king's eunuch, keeper of the women; and let them be given that which is necessary for their purification;

The sentence brought upon Vashti was that she could no longer enter into the presence of the king, and a new queen was to be selected.

It is very interesting that the Lord places the story of Esther here in the Bible as a special depiction of a parable about the end times that we live in. What was set in motion in Esther was done by a pagan king who, at the time, had absolutely no idea what he was really doing.

> 4 *and let the maiden which pleases the king be queen instead of Vashti. And the thing pleased the king, and he did so.*

Back in those times, much of this could have been very typical behavior for a king.

> 5 *Now in Shushan, the palace, there was a certain Jew, whose name was Mordecai, the son of Jair, the son of Shimei, the son of Kish, a Benjamite;*

The words translated *a certain Jew* have the connotation of being a freeborn Jew, not a slave.

Mordecai means "small" (the same meaning as *Paul* in Greek).

Jair means "he who illuminates."

Shimei means "he who hears."

Kish means "a bow."

Mordecai was a Benjamite who, with others from the tribe of

Benjamin, had stayed with Judah when the rest of Israel went astray.

This is the line of Mordecai, who is a representation of what the Holy Spirit does when he guides a person. In this entire story, Mordecai allowed himself to be led by the Spirit of God; he was illuminated by the Lord; he heard the voice of the Lord; he allowed the Lord to send him and move him.

Benjamin means "son of my right hand."

The right hand is the symbol of power in Scripture, but many Benjamites were left-handed. In Hebrew, a left-handed person is described as having their right hand impaired. The idea is that it is not by our own might or works or ideas, but by the Spirit of God. A left-handed "Benjamite" can walk with the Lord facing the same direction with his left hand in the Lord's strong right hand.

So here we have a very difficult situation. The Jews (mostly from Judah) had been sent by the Lord into a foreign land as slaves. God later stated that he had only been a bit angry (like King Ahasuerus) with them by sending them there, but the enemies of the people of God had taken advantage of the situation (Zechariah 1:15). Now, as the Lord was getting ready to correct this, the Enemy of the people of God geared up to bring about a final solution. The Enemy desired to kill all of them. He still does.

Throughout history, the Jews have suffered a lot of persecution and so have the Christians. An Enemy exists who desires to kill every Jew and every Christian. He is always seeking opportunity. He has not been able to do more damage because his opportunities have been limited by the hand of God. Even so, he keeps repeating the same mistake; he keeps overplaying his hand; he does not know when to quit.

5 *Now in Shushan, the palace, there was a certain*

> Jew, whose name was Mordecai, the son of Jair, the son of Shimei, the son of Kish, a Benjamite;
>
> 6 who had been carried away from Jerusalem with the captivity which had been carried away with Jeconiah, king of Judah, whom Nebuchadnezzar, the king of Babylon, had carried away.

Jeconiah means "the LORD establishes" or "the LORD raises up."

Scripture is very clear: It is the Lord who raises up or deposes kings. He can establish kings and kingdoms, and he can take them down. The leaders of the kingdoms of this world are subject to this. The Lord can raise them up or take them down.

> 7 And he had brought up Hadassah, that is, Esther, his uncle's daughter; for she had neither father nor mother, and the maid was fair and beautiful; and as her father and mother were dead, Mordecai had taken her for his own daughter.

Hadassah means "myrtle," which is linked in Scripture to the Feast of Tabernacles and the restoration of Israel (Zechariah 1:11; Nehemiah 9:15).

Esther's *father and mother were dead*. This is what happened to the entire human race.

God told Adam that in the day that he should eat of the Tree of the Knowledge of Good and Evil he would surely die. Adam and Eve died and death entered their entire line. All those who have been born since (with one exception) were born spiritually dead into a fallen and corrupt world.

When we, like this beautiful girl Esther, have been born into a fallen world in the midst of corruption and spiritual death on all sides, it does not mean that God has abandoned us. For Mordecai took Esther to be his own daughter. Mordecai is a symbol of the person who has been sent and is being led by the Spirit of God (John 3:34).

The Lord will become a father and a mother to the person who is seeking the light, to the person who is responding to the will of God. This will not just happen in the abstract, for God will also come upon the scene through a loving, caring person whom he has sent.

Choosing Esther

> 8 *So it came to pass, when the king's commandment and his decree was heard and when many maidens were gathered together unto Shushan, the palace, to the custody of Hegai, that Esther was brought also unto the king's house to the custody of Hegai, keeper of the women.*

Hegai simply means "eunuch."

Note that Esther did not volunteer for this beauty pageant. She belonged to a race that had been enslaved, and she did not yet know that the Enemy was also plotting to kill all of them.

Esther was caught up in this great pageant at the whim of a pagan king, just as Daniel and his friends had been captured and enrolled in a pagan religious school of Babylon. And God worked from there.

Many people wonder about this or that terrible situation that has happened to them. They think God cannot work in the midst of such problems and corruption, which continue to multiply before their eyes. However, they are very mistaken.

Many of the greatest stories of the love of God, the mercy of God, and the power of God come from this type of circumstance.

Look at this from the viewpoint of many religious people: This is a terrible story where the king took all the beautiful young virgins and slept with them one by one; he then put them in another house and never saw them again. And this poor girl, Esther, fell into such an awful trap.

But look at what God was about to do. Look at the test he allowed everyone (among his people) to go through. In the midst of all this, the king did not know that in figure, type, and shadow he was portraying an event of far-distant future times. He did not know that God was really using him. Esther was placed under the custody of Hegai.

> 9 *And the maiden pleased him, and she found mercy before him; and he speedily gave her that which was necessary for purification and her rations, and seven maidens, which were meet to be given her out of the king's house; and he moved her and her maids into the best place of the house of the women.*

Something similar happened to Daniel when he gained favor with those who were placed over him in an equally difficult situation.

> 10 *Esther had not declared her people nor her birth, for Mordecai had charged her that she should not declare it.*

If Esther had been able to consult with some of today's so-called experts regarding evangelism, they may have given her the opposite advice. Many new Christians are encouraged to let everyone know right away that they are a Christian. Most of the time this would seem to be good advice, yet it is essential that the Holy Spirit have the last word.

Gideon's experience was very similar to that of Esther. He and his men had to keep the light of their torches hidden inside their clay vessels until God gave the order to sound the trumpet, expose the light, and sound the battle cry.

> 11 *And Mordecai walked every day before the court of the women's house to know the peace of Esther and what was done with her.*

If we are walking with the Lord, it does not matter what happens; it does not matter if we find ourselves in seemingly terrible circumstances; it does not matter that we seem to be alone. The Lord is watching over us, and our peace does not depend on what is going on around us. Our peace depends on the Lord.

> 12 *Now when each maid's turn was come to go in to King Ahasuerus, after she had been twelve months according to the law regarding the women (for so were the days of their purifications accomplished, that is, six months with oil of myrrh and six months with aromatic odours and oils for women),*

The rites of purification for the Jews were different from these pagans. They lasted seven or fourteen days, whereas in this pagan kingdom, they lasted twelve months. Everything took place in the city called Shushan ("lilies").

There were twelve months of purification. *Twelve* is the number associated with childhood and with divine order. This is a necessary step to go beyond the law, which is linked to the Jews, and into the intermediate stage of young people, which is linked to grace (and to the church). Scripture defines three basic levels of maturity: children, young people, and those who are mature and may receive the fullness of their inheritance. This book has to do with the inheritance level.

Scripture refers to individuals as sons of God (regardless of gender), but women are symbolic of groups. Together we are the body of Christ, which is equivalent to the bride of Christ.

However, not all the "women" are the bride of Christ. We also need discernment regarding the king. Sometimes he represents God, and sometimes he represents the will of man (who is created in the image and likeness of God). It was God's desire for Adam to govern in communion with God. But this was lost; therefore, it is difficult (in this story) to know exactly who the king is, because, depending on the scene, sometimes he represents God, and sometimes he represents fallen man.

At the end of the story, however, restoration takes place. Just as the problem of the human race began with a woman who did not desire to obey and did not listen, the problem is solved with a woman who is willing to lay down her life.

In a very important stage of the development of this woman, she does not identify herself to anyone. No one knows who she really is except for Mordecai. This is a "woman" (congregation) that only the Holy Spirit can identify. Only those who are led by the Spirit of God can discern her.

She is not saying, "I am the representative of God here on the earth!" She is modest and humble and is in the midst of circumstances that are beyond her control – serious circumstances that are happening even now in many countries and among many peoples. Many are in grave difficulty, but God has his gaze upon those who are truly his.

The different "women" have the same opportunity, but some ask for one thing and others ask for something else. The Lord puts special people in place to care for this. Esther is not extravagant; she does not ask for one thing after another. She only takes that which is given to her by those whom the Lord has charged with this purpose.

First, seven maidens out of the king's house were given to Esther – seven maidens who were compatible with her. These maidens are symbolic of all those who are compatible with the same heart who will join her.

12 *six months with oil of myrrh*

The myrrh in verse 12 is symbolic of death and the way of the cross. The aromatic odors and oils in that same verse sound similar to the formula for the anointing oil in Exodus 30:22-33.

13 *then thus came each maiden unto the king;*

THE SEARCH FOR A NEW QUEEN

> *whatever she desired was given her to go with her out of the house of the women unto the king's house.*
>
> *14 In the evening she went, and on the morrow she returned into the second house of the women, to the custody of Shaashgaz, the king's eunuch, who kept the concubines; she came in unto the king no more, unless the king delighted in her and called for her by name.*

They only had one opportunity to impress the king. Many people do not understand that in the Christian life, sooner or later we will be tested, and we may only have one opportunity. These girls did not know when the king would call for them. They had to fulfill twelve months of purification, and then they could be called at any time. They had one opportunity. If the king did not like them, they would be taken to the second house and could never become the queen.

Many Christians think that by praying a certain prayer and fulfilling certain requirements, they will qualify to reign with Christ. This is not true.

Jesus Christ will return for a bride without spot or wrinkle or any such thing, but not all the "women" are like this.

The Scripture is very clear. Some will be wise virgins, and some will be foolish virgins. Some will enter into the kingdom with the king, and some will not (Matthew 25:1-13). The difference between the wise and the foolish virgins relates to whether or not they are connected to the source of the oil.

This is symbolized by the number twelve. It must be indelibly etched or marked upon the person.

> *15 Now when the turn of Esther, the daughter of Abihail, the uncle of Mordecai, who had taken her for his daughter, was come to go in unto the king, she required nothing but what Hegai, the king's*

eunuch, the keeper of the women, appointed. And Esther obtained grace in the sight of all those that looked upon her.

Abihail means "my father is power and my father is strength." God the Father was undoubtedly looking down upon her and giving her grace.

The eunuchs of the king are those who have a certain level of authority at the palace. Esther does not challenge them. She does exactly what they suggest, not more and not less.

This is key to how the king chooses Esther (and she does not challenge him either). Hegai knew the king. He knew what the king liked and what the king did not like. Esther had confidence in Hegai, so she went with what he gave her.

16 *So Esther was taken unto King Ahasuerus into his royal house in the tenth month, which is the month Tebeth, in the seventh year of his reign.*

The dates and numbers are extremely important here. They are symbolic of the events leading up to the Feast of Tabernacles. First comes the feast of trumpets on the first day of the seventh month of the agricultural calendar. This is the Jewish New Year on the sacred calendar. The Day of Atonement (or Day of Reconciliation) comes on the tenth day of the seventh month. Here we have Esther going in to the king on the tenth month of the seventh year. (It is curious to note that as I give this message, we are very close to being in the tenth year of the seventh millennium.)

The Scripture states that anyone who does not afflict their soul on the Day of Reconciliation will be cut off from among the people of God (Leviticus 23:27-32). It is very interesting that Esther made this preparation and was not cut off. The king received Esther and she was given the crown of the kingdom.

17 *And the king loved Esther above all the women,*

THE SEARCH FOR A NEW QUEEN

and she obtained grace and mercy in his sight more than did all the other virgins so that he set the crown of the kingdom upon her head and made her queen instead of Vashti.

18 Then the king made a great banquet unto all his princes and his slaves, the banquet of Esther; and he made a release to the provinces of their taxes and gave gifts according to the power of the king.

Esther's success was known and the results were experienced by the entire kingdom. Everyone received a blessing. This sounds a lot like the Jubilee (Leviticus 25).

19 And when the virgins were gathered together the second time, then Mordecai sat in the king's gate.

In Jesus' parable regarding the wise and foolish virgins, the second time the virgins are gathered occurs in Matthew 25:7-13. This is when the wise virgins entered into the marriage, and the foolish were left outside because their lamps were going out.

20 Esther had not yet declared her birth nor her people; as Mordecai had charged her; for Esther did the commandment of Mordecai as when she was being brought up with him.

Just like Esther and her circumstances, we contemplate the actual situation of what is happening in the world. What about North Korea? Many are concerned about Iran or Pakistan or Syria or Iraq or the Ukraine or so many other places or problems that surround us. There are potential nuclear problems and potential economic problems that could envelope the entire planet in catastrophe. Yet without a doubt, God has had his hand on the many circumstances regarding all these situations and has not allowed certain things to happen.

Yet we continue to wonder, what will happen?

Will a nuclear exchange take place?
Will the world economy go down?
What will happen?

One the one hand, we know that man is capable of destroying everything, but so far God has not allowed this to happen.

Scripture states that when the Lord Jesus returns, it will be like the days of Noah; it will be like the days of Sodom and Gomorrah. Even though in both cases there were many depraved, evil people who were causing a lot of trouble, when the end finally came, it was not the evil people that effected the collapse. It was the direct hand of God.

> *For as they were in the days before the flood, eating and drinking, marrying and giving in marriage, until the day that Noah entered into the ark.* (Matthew 24:38)

> *Likewise also as it was in the days of Lot; they ate, they drank, they bought, they sold, they planted, they built; but the same day that Lot went out of Sodom it rained fire and brimstone from heaven and destroyed them all.* (Luke 17:28-29)

Things are not going well in this present world, and all the forces of the world fight against one another. We are, however, coming to a time when change will happen, for Jesus told us a kingdom divided against itself cannot stand (Luke 11:17). God is about to do something as sublime and special as when Esther unexpectedly came on the scene into the kingdom of the Medes and the Persians.

> 20 *Esther had not yet declared her birth nor her people; as Mordecai had charged her; for Esther did the commandment of Mordecai as when she was being brought up with him.*

The Lord can lead us into many circumstances where it is extremely important to do exactly as he says. We are not to just repeat what someone taught us in some course or seminar. God knows how the difficult people of this world operate. We cannot win by arguing with them. The only way to convince them is to work and operate according to the ways of the Lord.

The religion of the Jews, what the Jews were saying, had not convinced everyone. They had only managed to make it so that many people desired to kill them. This is one of the main reasons that Mordecai told Esther to keep quiet.

Mordecai Saves the King

Esther now has the crown of the kingdom, but no one knows who she really is. Look at how this begins:

> 21 *In those days, while Mordecai sat in the king's gate, two of the king's eunuchs, Bigthan and Teresh, of those which kept the door, were wroth and sought to lay hand on King Ahasuerus.*

Bigthan (Bigtha) means "in his winepress," and *Teresh* is another name for *Carcas*, which means "severe." They were likely two of the same eunuchs who attempted to manage Vashti.

They wanted to kill the king and reign in his stead.

> 22 *And the thing was known by Mordecai; who told it unto Esther, the queen; and Esther notified the king of this in Mordecai's name.*

> 23 *And when inquisition was made of the matter, it was found out; therefore, they were both hanged on a tree; and it was written in the book of the chronicles before the king.*

Instead of being resentful about the way Esther had been snatched from her home and taken to the dangerous and complicated pagan beauty contest, and instead of being upset about how a nice, clean, Jewish girl had become the wife of a Gentile king, what did Mordecai and Esther do? They saved the life of the king!

The two culprits were hanged; everything was written down in the king's book; and apparently everything went back to normal.

This first stage ends with Mordecai seated in the gate of the king. This is where justice was served. Now God had someone with his Spirit with his foot in the door among the counselors of the king.

Let us pray:

> *Lord, we ask for understanding and for clarity that we not blindly react to the tempest that surrounds us, that we not respond with evil for evil, but that we respond only to your voice, to your heart, that we may embrace everything that pertains to you. Amen.*

CHAPTER 3

Haman's Hatred

Esther 3

1 *After these things King Ahasuerus promoted Haman, the son of Hammedatha, the Agagite, and advanced him and set his seat above all the princes that were with him.*

H*aman* means "magnificent."
Hammedatha means "double."
That Haman is an Agagite means that he came from the line of *Agag*, which means "I shall be the greatest."

Haman represents the old man, the descendants of Adam under the control and influence of the Devil who desires to control the earth in a way that is not the will of God.

The king, like all of us today, is capable of making decisions. Even though Mordecai, representing the new man (Christ), saved the life of the king, the king still promoted Haman above all the other princes.

This was a terrible decision, yet sadly, this is the predominant history of the human race. Adam and Eve received a paradise from God, but they soon made the wrong choice in which they ended up promoting someone similar to Haman.

The king represents many things in this book. The authority of the king obviously represents God, but God has created us in his own image and likeness. God has given each one of us authority. He gave Adam authority over all of creation, but Adam did what the king in this story did: He gave the authority (represented by the ring) to Haman (the Devil). From the beginning, the Devil has been trying to wipe out the entire line of the people of God (John 8:44). He knows that God said the son of a woman would crush his head, so he began killing the righteous, starting with Abel.

Here we have the history of mankind. The king represents each one of us who, like Adam, has been sovereign over something. Adam was sovereign over all of creation, and we are each sovereign over our own lives and over whatever additional responsibilities we have been given.

We can decide in favor of God or against God. We can decide for Haman or for Mordecai.

The evil intentions of those like Haman continue to this day. First, they desire for the whole world to worship them; then they attempt to eliminate all those who refuse to bow down to them.

> 2 *And all the king's slaves that were in the king's gate, knelt down and worshipped Haman, for the king had so commanded concerning him. But Mordecai did not kneel or worship before him.*

Mordecai was Queen Esther's uncle, whose name means "small." It is the same meaning as the name *Paul* in the New Testament.

> 3 *Then the king's slaves, who were in the king's gate, said unto Mordecai, Why dost thou pass over the king's commandment?*

> 4 *Now it came to pass, when they spoke daily unto him, and he did not hearken unto them, that they told Haman to see whether Mordecai's word would stand; for he had told them that he was a Jew.*

The word *Jew* came into use after the apostasy of the ten tribes in the northern kingdom. Before this, they had been known as "the nation of Israel," "the sons of Israel," and "the Israelites." Prior to the Babylonian captivity, however, the nation of Israel had divided into two nations or tribes. The tribe of Judah, along with the tribe of Benjamin and part of the tribe of the Levites, had been more faithful to God. The other ten tribes entered rapidly into idolatry, apostasy, and worse.

This is similar to the divisions that have occurred in the long history of the church. Scripture uses the term *Jew* to differentiate between the two and a half tribes known as the kingdom of the south (which retained their identity as Jews) and the tribes of the northern kingdom which completely disappeared. Even though the Jews were more faithful to God, they also entered into apostasy and were taken captive to Babylon.

The ten tribes were captured and dispersed and completely lost their national identity. The Jews, however, were taken to Babylon amidst many trials and tribulations, until God prepared the way for a remnant to return to Jerusalem.

This is also a symbol of the true believers within a church which in many instances has been taken captive by the system of this world, yet the Lord has always had a remnant. The Lord promises that at the end of the age he will have a clean remnant, a bride without spot or wrinkle or any such thing, and he will return for her.

We are seeing this happen today. We are living in a day when humanism dominates the churches, the nations, and the entities of the economic realm. The realm of the entire world has promoted and is worshipping "Haman." They have made gods out of outstanding, gifted humans, and these individuals have risen to the top of society until Haman has the ring of the king. He has the authority of the human race. Now everyone is required to bow and worship Haman.

> 5 *And when Haman saw that Mordecai did not kneel or worship before him, then Haman was filled with wrath.*
>
> 6 *And he thought it a small matter to lay hands on Mordecai alone; for now they had declared unto him the people of Mordecai; therefore, Haman sought to destroy all the Jews that were throughout the whole kingdom of Ahasuerus, the people of Mordecai.*
>
> 7 *In the first month, that is, the month of Nisan, in the twelfth year of King Ahasuerus, they cast Pur, that is, the lot, before Haman from day to day and from month to month,*

The conflict came to a head when Mordecai refused to worship Haman. The time came when Mordecai openly declared that he was a Jew. When everyone was forced to worship Haman, Mordecai refused. The grounds for refusal were that Jews only worship God and not man. This brought the previously hidden conflict to a head.

The book of Revelation speaks of those who receive the mark of the beast in their forehead and in their right hand (Revelation 13:16). The beast is the natural man. The mark in the forehead represents a certain mind-set or way of thinking, and the mark in the right hand represents a way of acting or doing things. This mark is required in order to be able to buy and sell. In order to participate in the commerce system of this world, a certain way of thinking and acting is mandatory (this requires the worship of "Haman").

Those who have the seal of God, which is the mind of Christ, are like Mordecai and they will not worship Haman or receive his mark (Revelation 7).

Haman believed in divination. He desired direction from the

occult world. He sought supernatural guidance to determine which exact day and month should be the time to exterminate all the Jews.

> 7 *and the twelfth month, that is, the month Adar was taken.*

They were in the first month, and the twelfth month *was taken*; therefore, Haman would destroy the Jews in eleven months. (It is curious that in Scripture the number eleven represents Christ.)

Haman presented himself to the nation as a type of false Christ, as the person who would cause the king and the people to prosper if everyone worshipped him. He wanted everyone to worship him. This is the meaning of *antichrist*.

> 8 *And Haman said unto King Ahasuerus,*

Haman had deceived the king, and the king was eating out of his hand. Many in power in the world today have deceived the human race and have people eating out of their hands. Scripture calls this generic problem the *spirit of antichrist*, and it has been functioning ever since the New Testament was written (1 John 2:18-27).

Scripture indicates that this problem will become concentrated, even though it is a problem of worship of the natural man, the old man. At the end of the age, this will center on one individual who will pass himself off as God upon the earth, and only those who are truly faithful to God will not worship him.

Scripture is also clear that the true Jew is not necessarily someone who belongs to a certain genetic race.

Romans 2

> 28 *For he is not a Jew who is one outwardly, neither is circumcision that which is done outwardly in the flesh;*

> 29 *but he is a Jew who is one inwardly, and circumcision is that of the heart, in the spirit and not in the letter, whose praise is not of men, but of God.*

The true Jew has a heart that has been circumcised and changed by God. The control of the old man, the old nature, has been cut. Those who are truly under the control of God and are moved by the Spirit of God refuse to worship man, and will not worship any specific man that may rise up.

There are many ways to worship and to pay attention to man, yet Mordecai refused to do any of it. Mordecai was a true Jew.

Haman's New Law

Esther 3

> 8 *And Haman said unto King Ahasuerus, There is a certain people scattered abroad and dispersed among the peoples in all the provinces of thy kingdom, and their laws are different from all other people; neither do they observe the king's laws: therefore it is not profitable for the king to allow them to remain.*

Haman told the king that he was going to exterminate an entire race that did not obey the king and that had their own law, but he did not tell the king that he was going to kill the Jews.

From Haman's perspective, something drastic had to be done in order to consolidate his magnificent plans for all humanity. (Today we do not speak of provinces, but rather of nations.) It is not profitable to allow this people who worship a higher power, who refuse to worship man, and who will not worship Haman, to remain.

> 9 *If it pleases the king, let it be written that they may be destroyed; and I will pay ten thousand*

talents of silver to the hands of those that have the charge of the public works, to bring it into the king's treasuries.

He does not even mention their names to the king. (And today will be the same. They will say, "We must do away with anyone who will not follow our grand strategy.")

Haman had the king's full attention. Then he decided to seal the deal with ten thousand talents of silver. One talent of silver was a lot of money; ten thousand talents was an enormous sum. Haman could offer this because he had control of the entire economy.

At the present time, somewhere, someplace, great plans are being made with a lot of money to consolidate power and control. The only things standing in the way are people like Mordecai.

If Haman is typical of the man of sin (the Antichrist), then Mordecai is also a personal example of the new man in Christ. Just as there may be individuals in particular in the end times who correspond to Haman and his sons, the same can also be true of Mordecai and Esther.

In Revelation chapter 11, there is reference to two witnesses of the Lord who face this desperate situation, clothed with sackcloth (symbol of repentance). They know that all the kingdoms of this world are against them, and they are in a war. It is the same scenario as in the book of Esther. What the Enemy attempts to do to the two witnesses is what happens in the end to their adversaries. It is a head-on conflict.

The Lord Jesus was the first one to face this system head-on. Many in Scripture symbolize the Lord Jesus, such as King David or Joseph in Egypt. Jacob was so happy with Joseph that he wanted another son like him, and so Benjamin was born. Mordecai is of the tribe of Benjamin. (Similarly, God the Father desires to have more sons, more individual members of the body of Christ who are a reflection of his Son Jesus. Mordecai represents this.) Curiously, when the rest of Israel went into fatal apostasy, many from Benjamin joined with Judah and with some of the Levites and the priests who continued to follow the Lord. This is where the word *Jew* comes from.

In verse 9, Haman offered the king ten thousand talents to be able to exterminate the Jews. Ten thousand is one hundred multiplied by one hundred (one hundred squared).

Another example in Scripture: *Three* has to do with fruit and *nine* with judgment. Three times three (three squared) is nine, and this is the effect or result of the law of the seed (we reap what we sow). One hundred is the plan of God and one hundred times one hundred is ten thousand. In Scripture, this symbolizes the reward for those who follow the plan of God. These numbers, however, can go one way or the other. *Nine* can mean the fruit (consequences) of righteousness or of unrighteousness.

Haman is offering the king ten thousand talents of silver. Silver is a symbol of redemption, but it can also represent greed.

Haman is a false Christ and is literally promising the king heaven on earth in exchange for being allowed to completely wipe out the people of God. Yet what will really happen if the system of man is fully implemented on earth (and if the people of God, whom Jesus said are the salt and the light, are eliminated) will be hell on earth. History bears this out. It has also been said that those who will not learn from the mistakes of others recorded in history are destined to repeat them.

Many have imposed the government of man along with the best ideas of man (and of man illuminated by demons passing themselves off as angels of light). This has not led to heaven on earth or to paradise, because human control, along with the control of the demons behind the natural man, is cruel and heavy. All systems of human control end up like this.

For this reason, we are not proposing any type of human system of government. We are not proposing another religious movement. We are not attempting to start yet another church in addition to all the churches that are already in existence. We are not proposing another human organization. We must directly follow the Lord like Mordecai and Esther did.

Then the Lord can join things together as he pleases. When the Lord joins hearts together, this does not result in an organization but in a living organism. This is the body of Christ; this is nothing less than the bride without spot or wrinkle or any such thing that he seeks.

Well, Haman made his pitch to the king and thought his closing argument was magnificent as he offered the king ten thousand talents of silver.

> 10 *And the king took his ring from his hand and gave it unto Haman, the son of Hammedatha, the Agagite, the Jews' enemy.*
>
> 11 *And the king said unto Haman, The silver is given to thee, the people also, to do with them as it seems good to thee.*

The king left everything in the hands of Haman.

> 12 *Then the king's scribes were called on the thirteenth day of the first month, and it was written according to all that Haman had commanded unto the king's lieutenants and to the governors that were over each province and to the rulers of every people of every province according to the writing thereof and to every people after their language; in the name of King Ahasuerus it was written and sealed with the king's ring.*

From the time that Mordecai heard this news, he had been

sitting clothed in sackcloth (symbol of repentance) at the gate of the king. The proclamation of this decree made on the thirteenth day of the first month was that on the thirteenth day of the twelfth month all the Jews in the entire world were to be exterminated.

The system of this world does not like those who do not worship man. Those who control the system of this world are seeking the right moment in time to fix this. There are also those who are behind the scenes controlling those who have visible control of the entities of this world.

What is really behind all of this? Who has such a mortal hatred for those in our present day, represented by Mordecai and Esther and are the true Jews?

The true enemy according to Scripture is not flesh and blood but spiritual principalities and powers of wickedness in high places (Ephesians 6:12).

Scripture insinuates that Satan will possess an individual, an important person. When this happens, he will attempt to bring his fractured kingdom together for a brief time. Scripture also states that someday Satan will be thrown out of heaven and will fall to the earth, knowing that his time is very short (Revelation 12:7-12).

Demons cannot really bring everything together because they fight fiercely among themselves. A demon doing one thing fights against another demon that is doing something else. However, when the Devil himself falls here on earth, he will attempt to intimidate everyone (including those of his own kingdom).

The Lord Jesus said that a kingdom divided against itself cannot stand. He was directly referring to Satan's kingdom here on earth (Matthew 12:25).

Scripture states that at the time of the end, the very elements of this world will be on fire (Galatians 4:3, 9; Colossians 2:8, 20; 2 Peter 3:10-12). In the highest sense, these "elements" are all the powers and dominions of wickedness (with the demons that are behind them) that manifest themselves through men and women who are like Haman and are presently running the world.

What I think will happen, what I see through the Scriptures, is that one way or another the Devil will wind up incarnate (inside a human being) here on earth. Then, after a brief period, he will be trapped and incarcerated inside what used to be his own jail of death where he had trapped so many souls throughout the centuries, because now Jesus has the keys to death and Hades (Revelation 1:18).

Scripture states that the Devil will be locked up for one thousand years, after which he will be released upon the earth for his judgment to be finalized (Revelation 20:1-10). Scripture also states that for the Lord, one thousand years are as a day (2 Peter 3:8).

> 13 *And the letters were sent by posts into all the king's provinces, to destroy, to kill, and to cause to perish, all Jews, both young and old, little children and women, in one day, upon the thirteenth day of the twelfth month, which is the month Adar, and to take the spoil of them for a prey.*

Haman gave very good incentives: Whoever kills a Jew may take whatever belongs to the Jew. They were to kill even the women and children.

> 14 *The copy of the writing was to be given as law in every province that it be published unto all the peoples, that they should be ready against that day.*

The diabolical plan for that specific day was ordained far and wide.

I am absolutely certain that the Enemy of the true people of God is planning something similar in our own day and age.

He is planning on using a given person and a group of persons in order to deceive the entire human race.

The human race was created in the image and likeness of God. This is why the human race in general is represented in this scene as King Ahasuerus. King Ahasuerus should be an image, a reflection of God. In some parts of the book of Esther, he is. But in other places, he is also the likeness of fallen humanity which becomes confused.

The king knew enough to choose Esther for her beauty, for her temperament, and for her humility – the characteristics of God that he could see in her. This is why he chose her, but he did not know much about her background and race. So Haman was able to deceive the king. Many people in the world are like this king.

These people respond favorably to those who are full of the life of God, are led by God, and are doing the work of God. Most people think this is fine, and they enjoy friendship with those who are like this without bothering to search out the background or spiritual trajectory of those in the world around them who are like Esther.

> 15 *The posts went out in haste by the king's commandment, and the law was given in Shushan, the palace. And the king and Haman sat down to drink; but the city of Shushan was perplexed.*

The king was drinking with Haman and the city was perplexed.

It is interesting to notice in this book that the Jews, after a long time in captivity and after hearing that the enemy had made concrete plans, authorized by the king, to kill them, all seemed to be kind of dazed and shell-shocked. They were almost at a complete loss as to what to do. Most of them seemed to think that the enemy would win.

Shushan is a symbol of the church, the true people of God in an intermediate stage of maturity (not pertaining either to little children or to fully mature adults). Later, when Mordecai comes into power, Scripture states that the city of Shushan rejoiced.

The servants of the palace who reported Mordecai to Haman did so because Mordecai said he was a Jew (that he belonged to God) and therefore could not worship anyone or anything else. The servants desired to see if Mordecai's word would stand.

Mordecai Mourns

Esther 4

1 *When Mordecai perceived all that was done, Mordecai rent his clothes and put on sackcloth with ashes and went out into the midst of the city and cried with a loud and a bitter cry*

2 *and came before the king's gate; for no one was allowed to enter into the king's gate clothed with sackcloth.*

3 *And in each province, wherever the king's commandment and his law came, there was great mourning among the Jews and fasting and weeping and wailing; and many lay in sackcloth and ashes.*

This was the reaction of all who were truly identified with the Lord. I suspect some pretended they were not really Jews so that nothing would happen to them.

In the first chapters of the book of Ezekiel, when Ezekiel sees the terrible abomination that is taking place in the Holy Place of the house of God (the Holy Place is symbolic of the present church of the priesthood of all believers), Scripture also states that many of the sons of Israel cry out and sigh as they see what is taking place.

So, what did God do? He identified each of these people by marking them with the mark of God (Ezekiel 9:4).

God is still doing this today. Those who are not in agreement with "Haman," who are not in agreement with the worship of man, which is taking place everywhere, including inside what should be the church of God, are crying out and sighing and showing genuine signs of repentance (sackcloth and ashes). These are the ones who are being sealed (marked) by God.

Early in Revelation 7, before any of God's judgments are initiated, those who belong to God are sealed with a mark in their foreheads.

Judgment is not always bad. Those who are evil will come to a bad end, but those who have a heart for God, are walking with God, and are planting good seed by the life of Christ within them will be rewarded in a just judgment (Revelation 11:18).

In Deuteronomy, Moses states that the blessing will come and overtake them (Deuteronomy 28:2). The steps of a righteous man are ordered by the Lord. They cannot be ordered by man (Psalm 37:23). Those who are ordering their own steps and think that they are fine, are not walking in righteousness.

Scripture also states that the wrath of man does not work the righteousness of God (James 1:20).

The true formula for blessing and prosperity is for us to walk in obedience to the Lord and allow our steps to be ordered by him no matter how difficult this may seem. Mordecai did not leave the king's gate. He could have hidden himself somewhere, but he chose to stay in the open and face the problem.

Mordecai continued to declare he was a Jew, he was part of the people of God, and therefore he could not and would not worship Haman. Each day Haman had to walk past Mordecai to pass through the king's gate. Now Mordecai was outside the gate instead of inside. The Lord Jesus depicts himself as outside the door of the church of the Laodiceans, calling to see if anyone will open the door and let him back inside (Revelation 3:20).

In our present situation, some people would like to flee the United States in an attempt to find a safe haven in some "neutral" third-world country in the face of the growing storm that threatens our horizon. They are wrong in doing this. We must face our present reality just like Mordecai did when he spent long hours each day sitting in the king's gate. Haman could not visit the king without walking right past Mordecai. If God's people lose their freedom in the United States, there will soon be no freedom anywhere else on the planet. We must make our stand at the "king's gate."

The very sight of Mordecai took away all of Haman's happiness. As long as Mordecai was there, Haman was not able to enjoy anything he had. Because of this, Haman did not want to kill just Mordecai; he wanted to wipe out all of Mordecai's people also.

The Devil attempted to kill the Lord Jesus, but this was not sufficient. He also desires to kill all the followers of the Lord Jesus, all those who have the same nature and life as our Lord Jesus, all of our brothers and sisters in Christ.

The king's commandment went out to all the provinces, and in each province, some reacted in the same manner as Mordecai.

Scripture is clear that these are the ones who will receive the seal (or mark) of God. This is clear in Ezekiel 9; this is clear in Revelation 7.

> 4 *So Esther's maids and her eunuchs came and told her. Then the queen was grieved exceedingly, and she sent raiment to clothe Mordecai and to take away his sackcloth from him; but he did not receive it.*

He did not receive the change of clothing. It was not the right moment.

> 5 Then Esther called for Hatach, one of the king's eunuchs, whom he had appointed to attend her, and sent him to Mordecai, to know what it was and why it was.
>
> 6 So Hatach went forth to Mordecai unto the plaza of the city, which was before the king's gate.

Mordecai was not in hiding, nor was he shouting; he was sending a message by his life and his example, like the two witnesses of Revelation 11. *Hatach* means "for sure," and he was a very reliable messenger.

> 7 And Mordecai told him of all that had happened unto him and of the sum of the money that Haman had promised to pay to the king's treasuries for the Jews, to destroy them.
>
> 8 Also he gave him the copy of the writing of the decree that was given at Shushan to destroy them, to show it unto Esther and to declare it unto her and to charge her that she should go in unto the king to make supplication unto him and to make request before him for her people.
>
> 9 And Hatach came and told Esther the words of Mordecai.
>
> 10 Again Esther spoke unto Hatach and sent him to say unto Mordecai.
>
> 11 All the king's slaves and the people of the king's provinces do know that anyone, whether man or woman, who shall come unto the king into the inner court without being called, by one law shall be put to death, unless the king shall hold out the golden

sceptre, that they may live; but I have not been called to come in unto the king these thirty days.

12 And they told to Mordecai Esther's words.

Mordecai's Charge to Esther

13 Then Mordecai told them to answer Esther, Do not think in thy soul that thou shalt escape in the king's house, more than all the Jews.

14 For if thou art silent at this time, then enlargement and deliverance shall arise to the Jews from another place, but thou and thy father's house shall be destroyed; and who knows whether thou art come to the kingdom for such a time as this?

Mordecai is telling Esther that in reality this problem is a great opportunity. This is the message from the Holy Spirit to all the Christians who are like Esther today.

15 Then Esther told them to return Mordecai this answer,

16 Go, gather together all the Jews that are present in Shushan and fast for me, and neither eat nor drink for three days, night or day; I also and my maidens will fast likewise; and so I will go in unto the king, even though this is not according to the law; and if I perish, I perish.

17 So Mordecai went and did according to all that Esther had commanded him.

Up until this time, Esther had always followed Mordecai's orders. Note the change here when Mordecai begins to follow Esther's orders instead.

This is interesting because Esther began by obeying the orders of Mordecai and the orders of the eunuchs of the house of the king (following their suggestions), so it would go well with her with the king. Now the time has come when everything begins to change, and Esther begins to give the orders.

This happened when she decided to risk her life and go into the presence of the king when the king had not called for her in over a month. She could have faced an immediate death sentence if the king had not extended grace to her in the form of his golden scepter. The king knew she had risked her life in order to make her petition.

When Queen Esther decided to do this, she gave a commandment to Mordecai and all the Jews to fast for three days prior, as she and her maidens did also. Scripture states that they fulfilled the commandment of Queen Esther.

Many teach that women cannot have ministry, that women cannot give orders to men. This is true under the law regarding the old man under the old nature in a fallen world. However, when we have new men (and women) full of the life and the presence of God (as part of a new creation), everything changes. In Christ there is neither male nor female (Galatians 3:28). The Holy Spirit may move through men or through women however and whenever God desires.

The same situation occurred in Shushan, with God moving through Mordecai until Esther reached a level of maturity in which she was willing to risk her life on behalf of her people. When she was willing to risk her life and go in to the king (even though this was not according to the law), she was qualified under the Spirit of God to give orders even to Mordecai (Galatians 5:18).

Is this not very interesting? Esther is not just any woman; she is demonstrating that she is not immature. She is seriously following the will of God and not acting on a whim.

The Lord has been working with his people throughout the

age of the church. He promises that after two (prophetic) days he will do something very special on the third day (in the third millennium since the first coming of Jesus Christ). The word that has come forth specifically for this time is:

"Do not feed your own life; do not use your gifts and calling for personal gain."

In the Old Testament, the true fast is explained in Isaiah 58. Under the law, the people understood that fasting meant not to eat food. But Isaiah describes it as living the life of the Lord as we deny ourselves, so we will be able to restore, liberate, and rebuild according to the ways and the nature of the Lord.

Physical fasting is an example that God can use, but the true fast is to not feed our own life. God desires to have a people who live like this in prayer and fasting. Prayer in this sense means an unbroken relationship with him in which two-way communication is ongoing and available at every instant. This type of prayer and fasting is not a religious exercise.

Man has turned fasting into something religious, and this allows religious spirits (demons) to manipulate many with feelings of guilt and shame if they do not participate in unending religious ritual. Or, if they do participate and excel, they are tempted and manipulated by religious pride that does not come from the Spirit of God.

If we desire to fast, we must make sure this is really of God. If it is, it should line up with what Jesus said in the Sermon on the Mount:

Matthew 6

> 17 *But thou, when thou dost fast, anoint thine head, and wash thy face*
>
> 18 *that thou appear not unto men to fast, but unto*

thy Father who is in secret; and thy Father, who sees in secret, shall reward thee openly.

Jesus also said that when we pray, it should be done in private and in secret. In fact, what we now call the Lord's Prayer was given in the context of Matthew 6:5-8 (that prayer, in order to be openly rewarded, should be done in private, even in secret).

Mordecai was like this. No one even knew that he was a Jew until he had to take a public stand and refuse to worship Haman. He was not a bad citizen, nor did he disrespect the king. He simply belonged exclusively to God and only worshipped God; therefore, he refused to worship Haman.

Queen Esther was even more reserved. She did not declare herself until the second banquet with the king and Haman. If she had not kept her secret until the precise strategic moment, God's plan would not have functioned properly. She managed to fast for three days without anyone in the palace finding out about it or asking the wrong questions.

As with Gideon's army, when they had the light but kept it hidden underneath clay pitchers until God showed them the right moment, Esther too followed a very precise battle plan.

Notice this:

When Mordecai went public and revealed that he was a Jew, the crisis began, because Haman became so infuriated that it was not enough for him to kill just Mordecai. No, that would be too simple. He needed to exterminate all the Jews. When Jesus came and declared himself to be the Son of God, the religious leaders united with Pilate and Herod to kill him. Ever since, there has been a worldwide, concerted effort against all of Jesus' kin.

Haman had to plan this well. He had to cast lots and have the occult world weigh in and choose the perfect date. He had to receive instructions from Satan and calculate how to trap the whole Jewish race.

Mordecai trusted the Lord completely because he continued to sit at the king's gate dressed in sackcloth and ashes. Anything could have happened to him at any time, but he had made a public commitment to stand for the Lord. He remained faithful with the same tenacity that Daniel had when he refused to pray to the king and continued to pray to God until they threw him into the lion's den. (Note: It is entirely possible that King Darius and King Ahasuerus are one and the same. See the explanation in *The Correction Factor*[2], page 10.)

Daniel's three young Hebrew companions had said, "It is possible that God will save us, but even if he does not, let it be known, O king, that we will not bow down to your image even if you throw us into the fiery furnace" (Daniel 3:16-18).

The Lord is forming a people like this today. It starts with individuals like Daniel and Mordecai, but now Esther represents a clean people willing to do whatever God desires.

Let us pray:

> *Heavenly Father, we ask for wisdom to discern the time in which we live. We ask for courage to not worship man, to not worship the old man, to not participate in the humanistic cult. May we be able to guard our secret and keep silent until you show us the right moment to confront the situation. We ask this in the name of our Lord Jesus Christ. Amen.*

---

[2] Russell M. Stendal, *The Correction Factor: Zechariah: A Key to Unlock the Book of Revelation* (Aneko Press, 2014), 10.

CHAPTER 4

Esther Risks Everything

All over the globe today, the natural man is seen as the solution. Political and spiritual leaders (not to mention actors, musicians, and sports stars) are being worshipped as demigods. The world still thinks that man can solve all of his own problems, when in reality things are getting worse and worse. The only ones who are not worshipping man are those who are being moved by the Spirit of God.

After Mordecai refused to worship Haman, it did not take very long for Haman to find out and plan a date to wipe out the entire Jewish race. This in turn triggered a decision by Esther to fast for three days. Queen Esther commanded Mordecai to gather all the Jews of Shushan and fast for three days. At the end of this time, she would risk her life on behalf of her people. We learned in the previous chapter that true fasting is when we do not feed our own life. It is when we depend on God's life (Isaiah 58).

On the third day (Esther 5:1), Esther entered into the presence of the king. Two thousand years (two prophetic days in which Scripture states that one day is as a thousand years) have passed since the first coming of the Lord Jesus Christ, since there has been a people of God like Esther upon the earth.

We are now entering the third prophetic day of God's plan. We are prophetically at the beginning of the third day mentioned by Esther. And "Esther" is approaching maturity in Christ. All her life she has faithfully followed the orders of "Mordecai" without questioning anything.

Esther 4

> 17 *So Mordecai went and did according to all that Esther had commanded him.*

Here we see Mordecai obeying the commands of Esther.

The Lord will have a people in this end time who do not seek to save their own lives. They seek the salvation of all of the people of God and are willing to lay down their own lives.

We will see that many who are truly of God will begin to meticulously follow the orders of this woman. Not only this, but before the end, even Haman will be obligated to obey her.

For Scripture states that every knee will bow and every tongue will confess (Isaiah 45:23).

God's plan is to have a queen that will have the same authority as the King because she has given up seeking her own will, and her sole purpose in life is to do his will. She has passed every trial and every test and has become a perfect complement to the King.

The Courage of Esther

Esther 5

> 1 *Now it came to pass on the third day, that Esther put on her royal apparel, and stood in the inner court of the king's house, over against the king's house; and the king sat upon his royal throne in the royal house, over against the gate of the house.*

This inner court corresponds to the Holy of Holies of the temple of God. The queen's royal apparel of fine linen, clean and bright, is the righteousness of the saints (Revelation 19:8).

If anyone were to enter the Holy of Holies in their own life, they would die. Only the high priest could enter once per year on the Day of Reconciliation (or Day of Atonement). This was the only way to enter the direct presence of God, and the priest had to come with blood that represents the life of Christ.

Now, however, our access to the throne of God is in the life of Jesus Christ; it is not in our own life.

Tests of our faithfulness can come in many forms as we face different trials where, in order to remain in good conscience, we must risk our lives like Mordecai and Esther. Some may have to risk their reputation; others will need to risk their capital or goods; and others may risk their physical lives. Esther was risking everything. She did this not once, but twice.

Our responses must become a lifestyle such that whenever we are in a critical situation that coincides with the will of God, we will be willing to put everything we have on the altar as many times as necessary.

> 2 *And it was so, when the king saw Esther, the queen, standing in the court, that she had grace in his sight;*

In whose sight? In the sight of the king.

But who does the king represent in this book? The king can represent God, but the king can also represent us who have been created in the image and likeness of God.

Even though God has ultimate power and authority over everyone and everything, he has also given us a will to make certain determinations regarding ourselves. We have the capability to promote "Haman," or we can give "Mordecai" and "Esther" the positions they deserve.

Most of the human race has seemingly good intentions, but even after recognizing the merits of "Esther," they still promote the worship of "Haman." Even while promoting Haman, the king (who in the broadest sense represents much of the human race in this example) is still seemingly oblivious to the fact that he is condemning the entire people of God.

The humanists of today (like Haman) do not really care about the people of God because the true people of God will not worship them; they will never worship them.

> 2 *And it was so, when the king saw Esther, the queen, standing in the court, that she had grace in his sight; and the king held out to Esther the golden sceptre that was in his hand. So Esther drew near and touched the top of the sceptre.*

This scepter or rod symbolizes the authority to reign and to govern. Gold can mean one of two things in Scripture. It can symbolize the nature of God, or it can mean the opposite in the life of the natural man. The New Testament declares that the love of money is the root of all evil (1 Timothy 6:10). Gold will represent one or the other – righteousness or self-righteousness.

The first time that the number 666 occurs in Scripture is during the reign of Solomon when the tribute from all over the earth that came to his kingdom was 666 talents of gold (1 Kings 10:14). This symbolizes all of the capacity and productivity of the natural man in the service of the kingdom of God.

In the book of Revelation, the number that symbolizes the mark of the beast is also 666. It is what should really pertain to God but instead is at the service of Haman.

This spirit of antichrist can operate in each one of us, although it seems that there will be a literal Haman at the end of this age. It appears that the Devil will be incarnate (in a human being) and must then be defeated and confined for one thousand years in what used to be his own jail (Revelation 20).

> 3 *Then the king said unto her, What wilt thou,*

> *Queen Esther? And what is thy request? It shall be given thee, even to the half of the kingdom.*

The king is conscious of Queen Esther and responds with grace. He desires to support her. He knows that she just risked her life to enter the throne room; therefore, she must have an important request. He is also beginning to understand that he is important to her.

Queen Esther is dedicated to saving humanity and having it restored to the image of God, but humanity cannot return to the image of God while Haman exists.

Sometimes the king represents us and sometimes he represents God (depending on each scene of this book). It has been God's plan from the beginning for man to be a worthy representative of God. This is where Adam failed. He sought his own benefit instead of remaining faithful to God and what God had placed under his authority.

> *4 And Esther answered, If it seems good to the king, let the king and Haman come today to the banquet that I have prepared for him.*

Esther knows that the Lord must order every step she takes. She knows that if we are to present the message of God to a person or persons who are dangerous, who may decide on a whim to take our lives, we must be extremely careful with our words.

When the Lord Jesus told the parable of the father who invited guests to a wedding supper for his son, he mentioned that the first invited guests refused to come and were disqualified; therefore, he continued to send out invitations to everyone.

The last invitation went like this: Bring everyone, bad and good, bring the maimed and the blind and the lame and compel them to come in (Matthew 22:10; Luke 14:17-21).

The Lord also orders us to give food and drink even to our

enemies (Proverbs 25:21). This is what Esther decides to do with Haman.

However, the Scripture also declares that a man was found in the wedding feast, among the invited guests, who was not wearing a proper wedding garment. This means that he was not found to be walking in righteousness. As a result, he was bound hands and feet and thrown into the outer darkness (Matthew 22:11-13).

The Lord says that in his kingdom he will remove all those who are not clean. And the only way to become and remain clean is to repent and trust Jesus to cleanse us so our heavenly Father will discipline and correct us as his sons.

Haman was given a great opportunity here; he had the opportunity to repent at the first banquet that Queen Esther invited him to.

> 5 *Then the king said, Cause Haman to make haste that he may do as Esther has said. So the king and Haman came to the banquet that Esther had prepared.*

The reaction of the king was to make Haman obey Queen Esther. Earlier we saw that Mordecai did all that Esther requested, so he had already been obeying the orders of Esther. Now Haman, by order of the king, also has to obey the commands of Esther.

But Esther still has not revealed who she really is. No one knows that she is a Jew.

The Lord has a people today who have not yet been revealed either. The first to be revealed are Mordecais. These are the individual sons of God and are not gender-specific. "Sons of God" may refer to men or to women.

However, when Scripture refers to the collective people of God, this is always typed by a woman, such as the bride of Christ (Revelation 21:9-10).

First, the individual sons must be revealed, and this will produce a terrible reaction in "Haman," causing him to desire to kill off the entire people of God. However, when his diabolical plan is set in motion, and our Enemy is fully distracted, the true corporate people of God (as typed by Esther) will be revealed. Satan has done this repeatedly throughout history. Hitler was no joke.

> 6 *And the king said unto Esther at the banquet of wine,*

Notice that she is offering wine (symbol of life) to the king and also to Haman. Notice too that the king is drinking the wine offered to him by Esther, and it is having a tremendous effect on him.

In Scripture, however, there are two classes of wine. One symbolizes the life of the old man (with the old wine). In the last pagan party of the kingdom of Babylon, the people were drinking the old wine out of the vessels of the temple of God (Daniel 5). Flesh and blood cannot inherit the kingdom of God. This was the end of the kingdom of Babylon. Cyrus the Persian and Darius the Mede (Ahasuerus may have been another name or a title for Darius) overthrew and destroyed the kingdom of Babylon that very night.

But the wine offered by Queen Esther to the king is the wine of the new life in Christ, of the grace of God. This has a different effect from one person to another.

> 6 *And the king said unto Esther at the banquet of wine, What is thy petition? And it shall be granted thee. What is thy request? Even to the half of the kingdom it shall be performed.*

Request?

Many people pray unto God with a petition, but in this

context a request is a bit different. The original word means "to demand."

If we place a petition before a judge or before a public official, this assumes that their response is at their discretion. However, a demand is not the same as a petition.

A demand, in this sense, is a legal requirement that must be resolved in favor of one party or the other.

The king offered Esther even half of the kingdom.

King Ahasuerus is head over heels in favor of Esther, but he still does not understand all of the implications of what is happening and the deception that Haman has wrought. King Ahasuerus caused the entire world to worship Haman, thinking that Haman was the solution, when in reality Haman was attempting to kill that which is most important to him.

> 7 *Then answered Esther and said, My petition and my request is:*

> 8 *If I have found grace in the sight of the king and if it pleases the king to grant my petition and to perform my request,*

The king knows that there is a petition and a request (really a demand). Esther uses the same terminology as the king. This petition has now become a demand.

> 8 *let the king and Haman come to the banquet that I shall prepare for them, and I will do tomorrow as the king has commanded.*

Tomorrow there will be another banquet.

If we look at this from a historic perspective, Queen Esther has been offering this banquet for two prophetic days – for two thousand years – and now we are at the end of this time period, so this situation will soon be resolved.

Haman's Plan

In the meantime, Haman has continued with his plan. Look at what he does between the two banquets:

> 9 *Then Haman went forth that day joyful and with a glad heart, but when Haman saw Mordecai in the king's gate and that he did not stand up nor move for him, he was filled with indignation against Mordecai.*

When the king grants the petition of Queen Esther, she hosts a banquet of wine at the palace and invites the king and Haman. In this first banquet, she does not reveal her true identity. She lets the king know he is very important to her and that she desires his presence.

The king and Haman have equal opportunity to eat the food and drink the wine that Esther offers. The king leaves the banquet with an even greater desire to do the will of Queen Esther. Haman leaves the banquet with an even greater desire to do away with all the Jews. He even decides to speed up the death of Mordecai by making a huge gallows, fifty cubits high, at the suggestion of his wife.

> 10 *Nevertheless, Haman refrained himself, and when he came home, he sent and called for his friends and Zeresh, his wife.*

Who is Zeresh, Haman's wife?

The Devil has a people just as God has a people. *Zeresh* means "gold," but "gold" in the sense of the insatiable desires of the natural man, instead of the nature of God. Zeresh is linked to self-righteousness.

The scribes and Pharisees who were in head-on conflict with the Lord Jesus also thought they were sons of Abraham and therefore sons of God.

Jesus told them, "If you were sons of Abraham, you would do

the works of Abraham. You are sons of your father the Devil" (John 8:39). In other words, if as individuals they were sons of the Devil, then collectively they would be the "wife" of the Devil.

Here these people are called Zeresh and are typed with the love of money which is the root of all evil (1 Timothy 6:10).

> 11 *And Haman told them of the glory of his riches and the multitude of his sons and all the things in which the king had promoted him and how he had advanced him above the princes and slaves of the king.*

One of the titles that Satan has in Scripture is the *prince of this world* (John 12:31). Satan is behind the prosperity of this world. Adam began the work of advancing and promoting Haman, and the vast majority of the human race has followed in Adam's footsteps.

The Devil attained his present position because of Adam and because Adam had been placed on earth by God as king. Adam could have reigned from the heart of God, but he chose to snatch for himself the knowledge of good and evil (after the Devil deceived Eve by telling her they would become like God).

This can happen to any individual. We are born into a fallen world and are infected with a mortal sickness. We are born destitute of the grace of God. We are born innocent but without the life of God.

Our natural reaction and predominant compulsion is to take whatever we can for ourselves. This places us under the control of the Devil who promotes the worship of Haman instead of the worship of God.

> 12 *Haman said, moreover, Even Esther, the queen, let no one come in with the king unto the banquet that she had prepared but myself, and tomorrow I am also invited by her with the king.*

The wine of Queen Esther brought out an accelerated attitude of pride and arrogance in Haman. On the other hand, the same wine caused the king to intensely desire to know and grant the petition or demand of Esther.

The gifts and ministries of God are not automatically revoked when a person falls into the clutches of the Enemy. Satan's gifts still function in the midst of his rebellion. But when he or his followers feed upon the things provided by God, his fundamental problem gets worse. His greed and pride and arrogance blind him and set him up for a fall. Judas went to the Last Supper with the other eleven apostles, but when Jesus fed him the bread dipped in wine, Scripture says that the Devil entered into him (John 13:27).

Haman (representing all those who operate like Judas) thinks that all the blessings he is enjoying (including the invitation of the queen) mean that he has God's stamp of approval. He does not stop for a minute to consider that God, through Queen Esther, is making an all-out effort to give him one last chance, and that all these wonderful things are really there to show forth the greatness and majesty of God.

In the midst of this, he boasts to his wife and to all his friends that *tomorrow I am also invited by her [Queen Esther] with the king*. All Haman can think of in his blinded state is:

> 13 Yet all this avails me nothing so long as I see
> Mordecai, the Jew, sitting at the king's gate.

It is important to note that Esther is serving the same food and the same wine to both the king and to Haman. Yet one is reacting in one manner and the other is reacting in the opposite manner.

Jesus compared the kingdom of God to a field in which both wheat and tares had been planted (Matthew 13:24-30). Both enjoyed the same sun and rain and soil, yet the wheat represents the sons of God and the tares represent the sons of the Devil. In the end, at the time of the harvest, a separation must take place.

> 14 *Then said Zeresh, his wife, and all his friends unto him, Let a gallows* [Hebrew *stake*] *be made fifty cubits high,*

The Hebrew word translated *gallows* is the word for "wood," "tree," "beam," or "stake" and is symbolic of the cross.

Fifty is the number of Pentecost, a number that also identifies the church over the past two thousand years, symbolized by the two banquets of Queen Esther. The true purpose of Pentecost is for God's people to be filled or submerged (baptized) into the Holy Spirit, so that by the Spirit we might put to death the deeds of the flesh (Romans 8:13). It is only by the Spirit of God that the old carnal man may be dealt with and eliminated.

The state of things here at the end of the age of Pentecost (the age of the church) is about as bad as things were at Shushan, the palace, in the twelfth year of King Ahasuerus. Other spirits are dominating vast sectors of the church and wowing the multitudes with supernatural events that are not holy. Haman has manipulated Pentecost to his own advantage and wants to use it to hang Mordecai, who represents those filled with the real Holy Spirit. In our modern era, Haman has almost succeeded.

God has allowed this untenable situation to continue because he desires to perfect us. He is able to cause all things to work together for good in the lives of those who love God and are called according to his purpose (Romans 8:28). God can use all of the persecution, all of the dangers, and all of those who would cause us damage to move us to depend more and more upon him.

Pentecost (meaning "fifty") has been the time of the gifts and ministries of God that were given to the church.

At the same time, Zeresh has been helping to convince Haman to hang Mordecai.

Notice this:

Haman used his influence with the king to sentence all the Jews to death on a certain future date, but then he found that his intense hatred of Mordecai could not wait until then (even though this date had been chosen and set by the use of divination).

Satan and Adam caused the entire human race to be sentenced to death, and so far no one (except Jesus Christ) has been able to escape this fate. The old man is sentenced to death and the only way for us to have eternal life is in Jesus.

Zeresh, Haman's wife, is well aware of Haman's obsession, so she helps accelerate his timetable for doing away with Mordecai. The sons of God who are nonconformists are such an obstacle to Haman that he precipitates his reaction and decides to kill them using the church system of Pentecost (the fifty-cubit gallows). Through the long centuries of church history, historians like George Foxe tell us that the Spanish Inquisition alone produced almost seventy million martyrs.

All of this is heading for a grand finale when the forces of evil will again attempt to completely do away with all the people of God. And again, this will prove to be futile. When they killed the Lord Jesus, God turned it around against the Enemy and brought about redemption for all of us.

All the strategy and maneuvers of the Enemy are in reality setting the stage for the final defeat of all the forces of evil.

> 14 *Let a gallows be made fifty cubits high, and tomorrow speak unto the king that Mordecai may be hanged upon it; then go in merrily with the king unto the banquet.*

Haman's wife told him to hang Mordecai, Esther's uncle, and

then go merrily with the king to the banquet that Esther had invited him to.

> 14 *And the thing pleased Haman, and he caused the gallows to be made.*

God has many sons, many individuals who throughout history have passed through many tests and trials and have come out victorious. But he has not had a collective people who have passed through these tests and trials and who have been able to manage power and riches according to the will and good pleasure of God.

And this is what the Lord will have. This is what is about to happen.

Let us pray:

> *Lord, we give you thanks for your light, for your life, for your wisdom, for your discernment. May we have discernment regarding the time in which we live. May we assimilate and live this message by your grace and by your Spirit. Amen.*

CHAPTER 5

Reward for Mordecai

Esther 6

1 *On that night the king could not sleep, and he commanded to bring the book of records of the chronicles, and they were read before the king.*

2 *And it was found written that Mordecai had told of Bigthana and Teresh, two of the king's eunuchs, the keepers of the door, who had sought to lay hand on King Ahasuerus.*

3 *And the king said, What honour and dignity has been done unto Mordecai for this? Then the king's servants who ministered unto him answered, Nothing has been done for him.*

4 *And the king said, Who is in the court? Now Haman had come into the outward court of the king's house to speak unto the king to hang Mordecai on the gallows that he had prepared for him.*

5 *And the king's servants said unto him, Behold, Haman stands in the court. And the king said, Let him come in.*

6 *So Haman came in. And the king said unto him, What shall be done unto the man whom the king delights to honour? Now Haman thought in his*

> heart, To whom would the king delight to do honour more than to myself?
>
> 7 And Haman answered the king, For the man whom the king delights to honour,
>
> 8 let the royal apparel be brought which the king wears, and the horse that the king rides upon, and the royal crown which is set upon his head;
>
> 9 and let this apparel and horse be delivered to the hand of one of the king's most noble princes, that he may clothe the man whom the king delights to honour and bring him on horseback through the street of the city, and proclaim before him, Thus shall it be done to the man whom the king delights to honour.

This uncovers much of what was in Haman's heart. It is apparent that Haman really desires the kingdom. He is not satisfied to be second to the king. He wants to be king. The Devil's strategy of humanism, getting people to worship themselves and human leadership, is just a front.

> 10 Then the king said to Haman, Make haste, and take the apparel and the horse, as thou hast said, and do so unto Mordecai, the Jew, that sits at the king's gate; let nothing fail of all that thou hast spoken.

Mordecai had spent a long time sitting in sackcloth at the gate of the king. Even though it looked like the king had not noticed him, he had definitely been brought to the attention of the king. The king also knew that Mordecai was a Jew because Mordecai had made a public declaration. The king was aware of much more than some people were thinking.

In a certain sense, Haman had pulled the wool over the

eyes of the king. However, the king was not quite as deceived as Haman thought.

This is also the case with our Enemy. Our real Enemy is a spiritual power of darkness who desires to do away with the entire race of the Lord Jesus Christ. He desires to eliminate all those who belong to the new man in Christ upon the earth.

Our Enemy has deceived humanity, causing almost everyone to worship mankind instead of worshipping their Creator. The natural man, however, is not quite as deceived as some would think. Many individuals all over the planet have become increasingly aware of "Mordecai." They are now aware that there are individuals (representatives of God) who are not participating in or going along with the cult worship of the natural man. These individuals are seemingly everywhere, in the gate of the "king," where the king can see them.

Who is the king?

The king represents each and every one of us, for even in our fallen, natural state we are created in the image and likeness of God. God has given each one of us certain sovereignty over our own life and existence.

All of us, however, have fallen short of the glory of God. As we have each sought our own interests, we have fallen into the hands of Haman (into the hands of the Devil), and the Devil has pulled the wool over our eyes.

But how far will this deception go?

In the book of Esther, the deception became very advanced. It appeared that there would be no escape for the Jews. It looked like Haman would be able to completely exterminate all of them. Haman had complete authority from the government. With this, he was able to obligate everyone to worship him instead of God. The only one who stood up and refused to worship Haman was Mordecai and a few friends of Mordecai who also dressed in sackcloth.

In the book of Revelation, two witnesses (Greek *martyrs*) of God are mentioned that prophesy dressed in sackcloth. This is in the context of a war fought in righteousness, because whatever their enemies attempt to do to God's witnesses comes right back upon their own heads (Revelation 11:5).

When Mordecai was asked to explain why he refused to worship Haman, he said that it was because he was a Jew (he belonged to the people of God); therefore, he could not worship anyone other than God.

This had to have made some type of impression upon the king. Maybe this was why the king was unable to sleep. Maybe the king was beginning to have second thoughts about the wisdom of having set up Haman as an object of worship for all the people. Maybe the king was beginning to notice the conflict between Mordecai (the new man in Christ) and Haman (the old man in Adam) and that it was Mordecai who had saved his life.

All those who are members of the new man in Christ (the body of Christ) have the Spirit of God. And who has always been behind the salvation of man?

The Spirit of God.

How did the Lord Jesus die for us?

Scripture states that the Spirit of God (the eternal Spirit) offered him up (Hebrews 9:14).

Haman's Humiliation

> 10 *Then the king said to Haman, Make haste, and take the apparel and the horse, as thou hast said, and do so unto Mordecai, the Jew, that sits at the king's gate; let nothing fail of all that thou hast spoken.*

All of the pent-up desires that Haman had to ride the king's horse, to be dressed in the robes of the king, to wear the king's crown, and to have proclamations exalting himself all over the city suddenly came tumbling down when the king unexpectedly ordered Haman to do all of this unto Mordecai the Jew.

> 11 *Then Haman took the apparel and the horse and clothed Mordecai and brought him on horseback through the plaza of the city and caused it to be proclaimed before him, Thus shall be done unto the man whom the king delights to honour.*

Jesus spoiled the principalities and powers. He made a show of them openly, triumphing over them (Colossians 2:15).

All of humanity is created in the image and likeness of God, and it is now the will of God to exalt those who are members of the body of Christ, who are part of the new man who will reign with Christ.

Scripture states that everyone will have to acknowledge this in the end. Every knee will bow, and every tongue will confess that Jesus Christ is Lord (Romans 14:11).

Christ is no longer a single individual. Christ is a body of many members with the Lord Jesus as the head (1 Corinthians 12:27; Colossians 1:18).

> 12 *After that Mordecai returned to the king's gate. But Haman hastened to his house mourning and having his head covered.*

The one who had been mourning at the king's gate was Mordecai. Now Haman runs home in distress, and Mordecai, strengthened and encouraged, resumes his position at the king's gate.

When Mordecai made his declaration that he could not worship Haman because he was a Jew, Scripture states that those who informed Haman of this did so because they desired to see if Mordecai's word would stand (Esther 3:4).

Imagine the atmosphere in the palace when the word went out that not only did Mordecai's word stand, but Haman himself had to conduct Mordecai throughout the city on the king's horse, dressed as the king, with the king's crown on his head, and proclaiming that this is how the king treats those whom he decides to honor.

This had to have been a serious blow not only to Haman, but also to whoever in the palace was undecided regarding the source and flow of the lines of authority in the kingdom.

> 13 *And Haman told Zeresh, his wife, and all his friends all that had befallen him. Then his wise men and Zeresh, his wife, said unto him, If Mordecai is of the seed of the Jews, before whom thou hast begun to fall, thou shalt not prevail against him, but shalt surely fall before him.*

Haman told his wife and his friends, because the Devil also has a corporate people upon the earth who are on his side. With his name meaning "small," Mordecai becomes an example of the least in the kingdom of God becoming the greatest (Mark 9:35).

The seed of the Jews relates to the Christ (the Messiah).

> 14 *And while they were yet talking with him, the king's eunuchs came in haste to bring Haman to the banquet that Esther had prepared.*

Haman did not even have a choice of whether or not he would go to the banquet. He was accustomed to giving all the orders, but things were now reversed. The king's eunuchs came and got him and made him go.

These eunuchs could have been some of the same eunuchs of the king who had been wondering:

Will Mordecai's word stand?

Will Haman be able to kill Mordecai and all of the Jews?

Will all the people of God be exterminated from upon the earth?

Let's look at this from another angle:

Many have been teaching that in the end times, in our present day and age, the great tribulation will come in which the Devil will take control of the entire earth, and he will do away with everyone who names the name of the Lord. (And just who do they think has been running the world system here on planet earth for the last six thousand years?) They fail to realize that even though intense tribulation throughout history against Jews and Christians has been caused by the Devil, the great tribulation, prophesied in Revelation 7-19, is caused by God, and before any of God's righteous judgments are poured out, those who belong to him are sealed and protected (Revelation 7:3).

Some, however, add a parenthesis and say that all the believers will be secretly raptured away straight into heaven years before Jesus actually returns and before any serious trouble happens. According to them, the Devil will win this round.

They teach that the Christians will be raptured into heaven for a certain period of time and removed from the battlefield here on earth, while the Devil will intensely persecute and kill the Jews that remain.

The Word of God says:

1 Thessalonians 4

> 16 *For the Lord himself shall descend from heaven with a shout, with the voice of the archangel, and with the trumpet of God; and the dead in Christ shall rise first;*

The Lord himself shall descend from heaven, and there shall be a lot of noise. This will catch those who are in darkness by surprise, as a thief in the night; but when it happens, it will be anything but secret (Matthew 24:26-27). The dead in Christ shall rise first in bodily resurrection before anything happens to us who are alive and remain.

> 17 *then we who are alive and remain shall be caught up together with them in the clouds, to meet the Lord in the air, and so shall we ever be with the Lord.*

The Greek word translated *air* means "lower atmosphere," because we will be caught up to meet him as he returns to the earth.

The word *rapture* is not in the English Bible. I do believe, however, everything the Bible says regarding those who are alive and remain and are *caught up* to meet the Lord in the air as he returns. I disagree with the use of the term "secret rapture," in which all the believers are supposedly removed from the battlefield here on earth and secretly disappear into heaven for three and a half or seven or even seventy years before the return of Jesus Christ as some are now teaching. Some even erroneously assert that the Holy Spirit will be removed from the earth during this time. In fact, the exact opposite is true. This is when the fullness of the Spirit will be poured out upon the body of Christ.

The Word of God holds open the possibility that the scenario of Queen Esther could unfold. God will have a clean people who will confront Haman and win. However, they will confront Haman according to God's way. They will operate like Esther and Mordecai.

What did Esther do?

She risked her life to invite the king and Haman to a banquet of wine. In the first banquet, she did not even mention the issue that was on her heart; all she did was tell the king that if he was interested, he could come back with Haman to another banquet.

At the second banquet, there was not only the invitation, not only the word of the king ordering Haman to comply with the commandment of Queen Esther, but also the eunuchs of the palace went to Haman's house and made sure that he would arrive at the banquet on time.

Scripture is very clear. God says that if our enemy is hungry, we are to feed him; if our enemy is thirsty, we are to give him something to drink (Proverbs 25:21). This is what Queen Esther has been doing, but the time has come for a confrontation.

The food and the wine of Queen Esther were having the effect of waking up the king more and more to the things of God. The same food and drink were helping to accelerate Haman into a losing strategy.

Esther is Revealed

Esther 7

1 So the king and Haman came to the banquet with Esther, the queen.

The king and Haman both arrived at Queen Esther's banquet, but they each symbolize a different group of people.

In Jesus' parable of the man who made a great supper, the man sent his servant to the highways and hedges to compel the guests to come in (Luke 14:23). Matthew says that they went into the highways and gathered together everyone that they found, both bad and good (Matthew 22:10).

The Lord also said that the kingdom of God is like a field in which the good husbandman planted good seed. However, in the night, while men slept, an enemy planted tares in and among the wheat. Both crops were allowed to grow up together until the time of the harvest when they would be separated. We are now at the end time of the harvest (Matthew 13:40).

The wheat and the tares have each brought forth fruit according to their nature. The wheat is giving forth the fruit of righteousness (justice), and the tares (the sons of the Evil One) are bringing forth their fruit based on lies, deception, and injustice, which will end in death and perdition (Matthew 13:36-43).

> 2 *And the king said again unto Esther on the second day at the banquet of wine, What is thy petition, Queen Esther? And it shall be granted thee. What is thy request? And it shall be performed, even to the half of the kingdom.*

The king reiterates that he is willing to share his kingdom with Esther because of the testimony that she has with him. We are now at the end of the second prophetic day as the church age is drawing to a close, because before the Lord, a day is as a thousand years and a thousand years are as a day (Psalm 90:4; 2 Peter 3:8). This is the second "day" when Queen Esther has invited the king and Haman to her banquet.

She has been feeding the king and Haman the same food and the same wine. Judas was served the same food and wine at the Last Supper as the other eleven. God causes his sun to rise on the evil and on the good. He sends rain on the just and on the unjust (Matthew 5:45). All of this continues until the time of the harvest. Then the fruit of each one is revealed. The fruit of the wicked is poison and the fruit of the righteous is food for the hungry (those who hunger and thirst for righteousness) and seed for the sower (those who are called to plant the gospel of peace).

> 3 *Then Esther, the queen, answered and said, If I have found grace in thy sight, O king and if it pleases the king, let my life be given me at my petition and my people at my request.*

> 4 *For we are sold, I and my people, to be destroyed, to be slain, and to perish. If we had been sold for menslaves and womenslaves, I would remain silent,*

even though the enemy could not recompense the damage to the king.

Queen Esther declares herself!

When Mordecai made his declaration and confirmed that he was a Jew, Haman decided to kill the entire race of the people of God. But when Esther makes her declaration and reveals who she is, it marks the end of Haman and the beginning of the end of all Haman's family and friends.

The second coming of Christ is not the return of a single individual. Yes, the Lord Jesus will return in person, but also as the head of a body of many members. He will return with and in and for a people without spot or wrinkle or any such thing. He will return with ten thousands of his saints (Jude 14). He will be leading the armies of heaven (Revelation 19:11-14). He will gather his elect from the ends of the heavens and from the ends of the earth, and his coming will be like lightning that is seen from the east to the west (Matthew 24:27). His second coming will catch off guard those who are not ready, as a thief in the night, but once Jesus is revealed from heaven (Revelation 6:14-17; 2 Peter 3:10; Isaiah 51:1-8), the events that follow will definitely not be secret. Those who are faithful to him here on earth will be caught up to meet him in the air and will also participate in his return (1 Thessalonians 4:13-18). Jesus will not allow his faithful remnant that is standing in the gate dressed in sackcloth like Mordecai to disappear. He will return to their aid bringing reinforcements.

Scripture also states that this man of sin (Haman) will be consumed with the Spirit of his mouth and removed with the clarity of his coming when he is revealed from heaven (2 Thessalonians 1:7; 2:8).

It is important to understand that the people represented by Esther are a corporate people and not a single individual.

It is also important to understand that Haman has a wife, he has a people, he has sons, and he is controlling all the forms of manmade government upon the earth.

> 5 *And King Ahasuerus answered and said unto Esther, the queen, Who is he, and where is he, that has filled his heart with the arrogance to do so?*
>
> 6 *Then Esther said, The man who is the adversary and enemy is this wicked Haman. Then Haman was afraid before the king and the queen.*

The king has become more and more certain of Queen Esther and what she is doing.

The Lord said that at the final banquet the last invitation was to go out to everyone – to the halt and to the maimed and to the blind, to the bad and to the good. The invitation is to those who are in the way and to those who are out of the way. Everyone is invited to put on a wedding garment and come and eat of the feast that God is offering. Every human being can be corrected, because the garment means coming under the authority of the Spirit of God, and the food is offered by the Lord to purge us, to cleanse us, and to prepare us.

The king has been feeding on the banquet of Queen Esther for two days. Being at the banquet of Queen Esther is not the same as drinking out there with Haman. This is what had happened when the king gave Haman his ring.

Scripture states that our adversary is the Devil (1 Peter 5:8). This verse insinuates that the Devil will become incarnate just like God became incarnate in Jesus Christ (2 Thessalonians 2:3; Isaiah 14:16).

The Devil wanted to kill Jesus. He thought he could trap Jesus forever in death. Things did not turn out, however, as the Devil planned.

The Lord Jesus broke the power of sin and death because he

did not come to do his own will. He came to do the will of his Father. Jesus was faithful to his Father unto death.

Scripture insinuates that the Devil will be subject to a similar situation, except the Devil will not be able to escape from the power of death.

> 7 And the king arising from the banquet of wine in his wrath went into the palace garden, and Haman stood up to make request for his life to Esther, the queen; for he saw that there was evil determined against him by the king.

Note that it was not enough for the king to accept Esther; he also had to reject Haman in order to get back to the "garden." Man was expelled from the garden of the "palace" of God because he chose to go against the will (law) of God. Scripture states that anyone who breaks even one statute of the law is guilty of breaking all of the law.

Adam's sin brought spiritual death upon all of his descendants except one. The only human not born spiritually dead after Adam was our Lord Jesus, who was begotten by the Word of God and born of Mary.

As soon as the king sees Haman for who Haman really is and rejects him, he returns to the garden of the palace.

Why were Adam and Eve banished from the garden of God?

This happened because they believed the word of the Devil more than the word of God.

What had God said?

God told Adam not to eat of the fruit of the Tree of the Knowledge of Good and Evil because in the day that he would eat of it, he would surely die. The lie of the serpent unto Eve was that she would not die if she disobeyed God. He claimed that if she ate of the forbidden tree, she would become like God. He said God did not want them to become like him, so he prohibited them from eating such wonderful fruit. But the serpent told them to eat and their eyes would be opened. Eve believed the Devil instead of believing the word of God given to her by Adam, her husband.

When the king finally understands that the long-term strategy of the Devil for all this time has been to destroy all the people of God while exalting himself above the throne of God, and when it fully dawns on the king that Haman has only been concerned with exalting himself and that he is the mortal enemy of Esther and of her people, then the king will return to the garden of God. He will once again believe the Word of God and will desperately seek the presence of God. It is not enough to desire to share his kingdom with Esther. In order to return to the peace of the presence of God, the king must be willing to give up Haman and surrender all of his kingdom authority to Esther and Mordecai. These are the essential conditions of the Day of Reconciliation (Yom Kippur or Day of Atonement). The Feast of Tabernacles is now at hand (Leviticus 23:23-44).

From this point on, there is virtually no difference between what the king does and what we would expect the Lord Jesus Christ to do if he were here in person. This is evidence of total conversion; this is evidence that the king now has the heart of God.

God has placed authority in man, but this is one reason we can become confused regarding the word *angel*. In general usage, an angel is a celestial being that is different from the human race, and many angels exist in this sense of the word. However, the word for *angel* in the Hebrew Scriptures can also apply to people like us if we comply with and fulfill the will of God.

The word *Malachi* in Scripture means "my angel." Scripture uses the word *angel* many times to refer to human beings like us who live to do the will of God instead of our own will. God's desire from the beginning was to have human beings who would represent him as he is.

The angels, such as cherubim and seraphim, represent him in some way, yet even among them, the third part followed Satan (Revelation 12:3-4). However, the Lord did something regarding man that he did not do with the angels: He not only gave man sovereignty over his own life, but also over this earth. Man, however, ceded this authority to Satan.

Now there is a race of men of which Mordecai is a symbol – those who are born again in the life of the Lord Jesus Christ and have not yielded to Satan. They have not bowed to any of those who follow Satan. This is where Satan's problem lies. This is a direct threat to Satan and the reason for the great conflict that is presently raging.

Hanging of Haman

> 7 And the king arising from the banquet of wine in his wrath went into the palace garden, and Haman stood up to make request for his life to Esther, the queen; for he saw that there was evil determined against him by the king.

Many mistakenly think that the events surrounding the first coming of our Lord Jesus Christ were sufficient to condemn Haman (Satan). And yes, they were sufficient to effect God's plan of redemption and salvation for all of mankind. But under the Law, two or three witnesses are required to condemn anyone to death for rebellion and murder (Deuteronomy 17:6).

The Scripture states that Jesus Christ is a faithful witness (Greek *martyr*), but a victorious people of God act as the second witness. Without the testimony of "Esther," it is impossible to condemn "Haman."

Queen Esther represents a clean people of God, but the

Devil is the accuser of the brethren (Revelation 12:10). If he encounters valid grounds to accuse us, he can subvert our testimony against him.

If we claim to be the people of God, the bride of Christ, and members of the body of Christ, but live as hypocrites with unclean lives, our testimony is not valid. Jesus is coming back for a bride without spot or wrinkle or any such thing (Ephesians 5:27). Revelation 11 describes the events that will occur when there are two witnesses instead of one.

> 8 Then the king returned out of the palace garden into the place of the banquet of wine, and Haman had fallen upon the bed upon which Esther was. Then said the king, Will he force the queen also before me in the house? When this word went out of the king's mouth, they covered Haman's face.

Haman panicked. He is desperate to save his life and does not know what to do now that both the king and the queen are against him.

Haman got too close to the queen in his desperate attempt to save himself. Now the king can see with his own eyes, in addition to the testimony of Esther, that Haman has no respect for the queen.

> 9 Then said Harbonah, one of the eunuchs before the king, Behold also, the gallows [Hebrew *stake*] fifty cubits high, which Haman had made for Mordecai, who had spoken good for the king, stands in the house of Haman. Then the king said, Hang him upon it.

The Hebrew word for *gallows* is the same word that would apply if referring to a cross. Essentially the same thing will happen to Haman (the Devil) as what the Devil did to Jesus.

Harbonah means "ass herder."

There was much "ministry" going on in the house of the king, but some of it may not have been so tender. This eunuch apparently knew how to herd "asses."

Harbonah had been observing this situation develop. He must have heard Mordecai from the beginning. He had been wondering if the word of Mordecai would stand.

Now Harbonah decides to see this through to the end. He has a key role, yet as a servant of the king, he does not leap to judgment and say, hang him. He tells the king that Haman had built a gallows to hang Mordecai on. Harbonah must have seen the gallows when he went to bring Haman to the queen's banquet. He reminded the king that Mordecai was the one who had spoken up and saved the life of the king.

They sent the ass herder, Harbonah, to bring Haman to the second banquet. The king knew who would be the right servant to send. The king was not quite as deceived as one may think. He knew enough to have someone like Harbonah standing by during the banquet just in case his services should be needed. The truth about Haman had been gradually dawning on the king. Instead of Haman being a sublime, magnificent intellectual as he had first thought, the king realized he may have been mistaken, and Haman might really be a wild ass.

Revelation 20 states that when the time comes, all the Lord has to do is to send one angel to bind the Devil with a chain and cast him into the bottomless pit that represents the first death.

They had thought that Haman was (and his name means) magnificent. He appears on the surface to be magnificent (this is how Eve perceived the Devil). He appears to be a great intellectual who has the explanation for everything. Many of the elites of this world believe this about themselves. Scripture states, however, that the day will come when the Devil (and his followers) will be revealed for what they are, and the onlookers will say:

Is this the man who caused so much trouble?

Is this the man who placed the entire world into conflict?

Is this the man behind so many wars and so much death and so much oppression and slavery?

He will be revealed as insufficient and useless and will be imprisoned by death for one thousand years (Isaiah 14, Revelation 20).

We are approaching the time in history when it behooves the king to have Harbonah (that servant or angel who knows how to handle asses) close at hand (Revelation 20:1).

10 So they hanged Haman on the gallows that he had prepared for Mordecai. Then the king's wrath was pacified.

When this happens, the human race will once again be free. This can happen both on an individual level as well as on a collective level. Each and every one of us needs to make the decision to agree with Esther and Mordecai and, like the king, make the decision to hang Haman.

A man of sin desires to sit on the throne of each and every one of our lives. He will only be destroyed and removed by the presence of the Lord. There will also be a grand finale that will soon take place on the stage of the entire world.

"Haman" still dominates the world stage, and it still appears as though he may be successful in exterminating the people of God from the earth. The desire of Haman and his people is to completely destroy all the people of God. Our enemies, however, have made one mistake after another. They had (and have) a plan and they have a set date when they plan to take action on a worldwide basis. We know that the date is drawing near, but we also know that some like Mordecai will never bow and worship man or any unclean evil spirit that may be hiding behind a natural man.

All of these who are like Mordecai together form a people

of God that is like a clean woman. This is the bride for which the Lord Jesus will return.

Mordecai Receives the Ring

Esther 8

> 1 *On that same day King Ahasuerus gave the house of Haman, the Jews' enemy, unto Esther, the queen. And Mordecai came before the king, for Esther had told what he was unto her.*
>
> 2 *And the king took off his ring, which he had taken from Haman and gave it unto Mordecai. And Esther set Mordecai over the house of Haman.*

This has not yet taken place in actual practice on the world scene, but the time is close. And this scenario will continue and continue and continue. The King's dominion and peace shall have no end (Isaiah 9:7).

When Haman was in charge, many people were not really converted and had chosen to distance themselves from the people of God. They thought the people of God were going to come to a bad end. However, when the situation suddenly turns around, they begin to have second thoughts.

Esther had risked her life on two separate occasions to enter the private throne room of the king. This led to two banquets and ended with the king doing whatever Esther desired.

What does Queen Esther really desire?

That Mordecai be put in charge of everything concerning the kingdom.

Along the way, the enemies of the Jews began to have ever-increasing fear and respect for Mordecai and Esther.

The new law that they establish and seal with the king's signet ring is not a law for them to do whatever they want. It is simply a law allowing the Jews to defend themselves from their enemies.

What happens to the enemies is exactly what the enemies were planning to do to the people of God!

Today, for us to escape the problem represented by Haman, the queen – the true people of God – must be tested to determine the true state of their hearts. She must be willing to risk her life for her people; she must be willing to follow the direct instructions of God in all things.

Esther did not consult Mordecai regarding the two banquets that she prepared. She followed her pure heart and knew what to do because she was not seeking her own life. She attended to the king and to Haman, and God took care of the rest. God provided the precise moment for her to be revealed, and the day and the hour that she was revealed was the end of Haman.

The end of Haman was the beginning of another age.

The law of sin and death cannot be undone; not a jot or a tittle of the law can be undone until everything is fulfilled (Matthew 5:17-20). There is, however, another law – the law of the Spirit of life in Jesus Christ (Romans 8:2). This is the law that dominates the people of Esther, because those who are led by the Spirit are not under the law (Galatians 5:18). The Spirit trumps the law of sin and death!

We have passed through a very long time (two prophetic days) when those who are true to God have only been able to dress in sackcloth in the face of the events going on in the world around them. We are, however, rapidly approaching the time when the ring will be taken from the finger of Haman and returned into the hands of the king. This time the king will place the ring upon the finger of Mordecai, and Mordecai will have the authority to straighten things out.

Scripture does not specify exactly when this will take place. In fact, it says that no one will know the day or the hour. The apostle John wrote what he saw in the book of the Revelation of Jesus Christ because this revelation is the manifestation of the fullness of Christ in a body of many members, of which Jesus Christ is the Head.

The apocalyptic events mentioned in Revelation have to do with the natural man and everything that has been corrupted and contaminated by him that must be destroyed. The Revelation is the restoration of the life and the garden of God far exceeding what Adam and Eve lost. This is nothing less than new heavens and a new earth (Isaiah 65:17; 2 Peter 3:13).

This is the result of the ministry of Mordecai and Esther. This is the result of the human race coming back into compliance with the will of God.

Many think that when the Devil is trapped by death for one thousand years and chained in the bottomless pit (in Hades), everything on earth will automatically become perfect. This is not the case.

Conflict will continue, but it will be different because the people of God will have the right to defend themselves. They will be allowed to defend themselves because they are not seeking their own good.

This story is not over, however. The Devil is not the last enemy; many enemies exist in addition to the Devil. Scripture is clear that the last enemy that must be overcome is death (1 Corinthians 15:26). Death is the result of corruption and sin (Romans 6:23).

After the Devil is overcome and locked up, no one will be able to blame the Devil for his or her bad behavior. Then the motives of each one will be revealed, and those who claim to belong to God will be faced with another and possibly even greater test.

What will that test be?

It will be the test of power and of riches. It will be the test of prosperity. This will be the test that the Devil himself was unable to overcome.

He had everything: He was very close to God and he had a lot of responsibility, yet he became angry because God put the earth under the responsibility of Adam. Lucifer became obsessed with having authority over the earth, and as he attempted to elevate himself, he fell (Isaiah 14:12-15).

And the third part of the heavenly hosts fell with him. After they fell, nothing more could be done for them. It was not possible to evangelize them with the good news of the gospel; it was not possible to tell them anything more about the goodness of God that they did not already know. They had full knowledge and experience of all of this and even so, turned their backs upon God; therefore, when they fell, it was not possible to bring them to repentance, for God closed this door (2 Peter 2:4; Jude 6).

God allowed their rebellion to continue for six thousand years. Why?

Because God in his infinite wisdom saw a great opportunity in all of this.

The angels were created to worship God; they lived in the direct presence of God; and when they fell, there was no way to redeem them. On the other hand, when humankind after Adam was born into spiritual darkness, born as slaves into a corrupt and fallen world where the Devil has authority, they would have the possibility of being redeemed. They would have the possibility of God offering them his plan of redemption, of God reaching out his hand to them, and those that would respond to God's initiative would find life and salvation.

Those who come out of this type of darkness are as though they were vaccinated against evil. They no longer have any desire to follow the Devil, and they are able to see something that was not all that clear to Adam and Eve (or to the angels that fell). They can see that the Word of God will stand forever

(Isaiah 40:8) and the fear of the Lord is wisdom (Job 28:28). They can see that the life of God, the life that God breathed into Adam in the beginning, is priceless; it is something that we do not deserve. They can see that our natural life without God is nothing compared to this.

In the midst of all the darkness, strife, and corruption (due to the fall), God results with those who appreciate him for who he really is. God results with true friends who have made difficult choices to follow him and stay with him against all odds and not just because things have always been this way (as was the case with Adam and Eve before the fall). In the midst of all the trouble and confusion of a fallen creation, God can still choose people like us, and we can still choose to respond to his call and follow him.

The Lord has been able to extract much good out of the wicked plan and scheme of Satan (of Haman), for all things work together for good for those that love the Lord and are called according to his purpose (Romans 8:28).

The Scriptures state that even the angels that did not fall look upon us with fervent attention, because what God is doing with human beings like us is of great interest to them (1 Peter 1:12). This teaches them things that they did not know, and they are seeing a side of God that they did not previously understand perfectly. Scripture also implies that God is preparing something for us, a new creation where we will reign with Christ even above the angels (1 Corinthians 6:3).

The angels in the highest sense are servants of God, but the plan of God is for us to become sons of God (Hebrews 2:14-18). We are offered a place within the very family of God as brothers and sisters, as joint-heirs with Christ (Romans 8:17; Ephesians 3:1-6).

Let us pray:

Lord, we do not seek just wisdom and understanding, but also revelation of who you really are. Please reveal your character and your life in us. Amen.

Chapter 6

Esther's Plea

Esther 8

1 *On that same day King Ahasuerus gave the house of Haman, the Jews' enemy, unto Esther, the queen. And Mordecai came before the king, for Esther had told what he was unto her.*

2 *And the king took off his ring, which he had taken from Haman and gave it unto Mordecai. And Esther set Mordecai over the house of Haman.*

Queen Esther represents a true people of God – a people of God who begin their service to God by obeying everyone the Lord has placed in their path. Mordecai is a symbol of the Spirit of God and of the way that the Holy Spirit works through those whom God establishes.

Even though Mordecai is very visible and predominant, Esther is the one who wins this battle. Mordecai is afflicted. He reveals himself. He announces his position and his word is firm. Mordecai represents all of the sons of God who, as individuals, must take a firm position in reference to that which is happening in the world around us.

We cannot worship the natural man. We cannot worship those who manage this world under the governments of the god of this age, the Devil (2 Corinthians 4:4).

Queen Esther, as a woman, represents all of the clean people of God. The Lord will return for a clean bride. Scripture also states that we are all members of the body of Christ of which he is the Head. This is the people of God, united, clean, and obedient, who will win this battle.

Queen Esther begins by following the orders of Mordecai and others, but she wins by following orders directly from God, as the Spirit of God moves in her heart. Only God could reveal the details of how to manage her behavior towards the king and tell her what to do at the last banquet. Only God could show her how to reveal who she was in a manner that would bring about the overthrow and death of Haman and trigger a chain of events that would bring total victory for her and for her people.

It is interesting to note that the king does not give the house and estate of Haman directly to Mordecai. He gives it to Esther, and she places it under the administration of Mordecai.

> 2 And the king took off his ring, which he had taken from Haman and gave it unto Mordecai.

The king gave his ring, his authority, unto Mordecai.

> 2 And Esther set Mordecai over the house of Haman.

Now we have both the king and the queen fulfilling their functions.

The book of Revelation ends on this note: *And the Spirit and the bride say, Come. . . . And let him that is thirsty come; and whosoever will, let him take of the water of life freely* (Revelation 22:17).

Notice that the Lord will have a bride that will do exactly as he is doing, and she will have great authority in his house.

> 3 And Esther spoke yet again before the king and fell down at his feet and besought him with tears to put away the evil of Haman, the Agagite, and his device that he had devised against the Jews.

> 4 *Then the king held out the golden sceptre toward Esther. So Esther arose and stood before the king,*

She went before the king a second time without being invited and again risked the death penalty. And again, the king extended the golden scepter.

> 5 *And said, If it pleases the king and if I have found grace in his sight and if the thing is right before the king and if I am good in his eyes, let it be written to reverse the letters devised by Haman, the son of Hammedatha, the Agagite, which he wrote to destroy the Jews who are in all the king's provinces.*
>
> 6 *For how can I endure to see the evil that shall come unto my people? How can I endure to see the destruction of my nation?*

It is important to understand the magnitude of the failure of King Saul when he disobeyed the command of the Lord to kill King Agag (1 Samuel 15). Haman was a descendant of Agag, king of the *Amalekites* (meaning "strangers"). These people represent the natural man who has declared himself against God and has willingly joined the Enemy.

The natural man will not be saved. Salvation is in Christ in the new man, not in the old man. Those who insist on saving the old man wind up challenging God because this is not the plan or purpose of God (Matthew 7:21-23).

King Saul killed all that he considered evil and saved what he thought was good for himself. God rejected Saul from that day forward, and the Holy Spirit that was upon Saul left. Saul did not even seem to be aware of when that happened (1 Samuel 16:14-15).

The Spirit of God was working in and through Esther, and this began to affect the heart of the king. Over time, this process caused the king to become 100 percent in favor of Esther and Mordecai.

The Song of Solomon ends with the Shulamite (who spiritually represents the same woman as Esther) giving orders to the companions in the house of the king. Finally, even the king hearkens to what she says (Song of Solomon 8:13).

Why?

Because she has demonstrated that her inheritance is the king and she is his inheritance. She represents a people of God who will not ask amiss. They will make their petitions according to the will of God, not to seek their own good. They are willing to lay down their lives for God and for the people of God.

The New Law

> 7 Then King Ahasuerus said unto Esther, the queen, and to Mordecai, the Jew, Behold, I have given Esther the house of Haman, and they have hanged him upon the gallows because he extended his hand against the Jews.
>
> 8 Write ye also for the Jews, as it pleases you, in the king's name, and seal it with the king's ring; for the writing which is written in the king's name and sealed with the king's ring may not be revoked.

The king tells them to write a new law, because the law that Haman wrote and sealed with the ring of the king could not be revoked.

Romans 8 speaks of two laws that apply to all of humanity and which coincide with this example. One is called the law of sin and death. This law was given when the nation of the people of God chose to save their own lives. They said unto Moses, "Speak thou with us, and we will hear; but let not God speak with us lest we die." They felt that if they were to draw near to that mountain and continue to hear the voice of the Lord, they would die. They wanted Moses to go up and listen to God and then come back and tell them what he said (Exodus 20:19).

This is how they obtained a law written on tablets of stone (and they had thoroughly broken this law even before Moses was able to come down the mountain and show it to them). The desire of God has always been to write his laws on the tablets of our hearts and in our minds (Jeremiah 31:33). He desires to change the very nature of man, but for this to happen, man must be willing to let go of his own life. Under the law of sin and death, which was given unto Moses, whoever failed to comply with even one point was guilty of breaking the entire law and would come under the curse (James 2:10).

In the New Testament, Paul writes that we have all sinned and are made destitute of the glory of God and that each one is guilty of selfishly seeking his own good (Romans 3:23). Everyone is under a sentence of death, a death sentence like what Haman decreed over the entire nation of the Jews.

When the second law is given, which is the law of life in the Spirit, the first law is not done away with. Jesus clearly stated that he did not come to abolish the Law or the prophets. Instead, he came to give them their true fulfillment (Matthew 5:17).

The only way to give the true fulfillment is by the path prefigured by Mordecai and Esther. This happened when Mordecai declared himself and risked his life by refusing to worship Haman, who responded with a death sentence for Mordecai and his people. When Esther entered into the presence of the king, she was risking her life. She was showing the king that she was not attached to her own life.

The Lord Jesus did not come to undo the law of sin and death (Matthew 5:17). He did not proffer some magic formula. He did not leave mankind as corrupt sinners with their selfish nature intact to be saved simply by repeating a prayer or participating in religious rites and rituals. No!

The Lord Jesus came to demonstrate the way unto death; he came to overcome death. He came so the law might be fulfilled in him. He fulfilled the law that would have trapped any of us in death, in Sheol or Hades (which was a type of jail managed by the Devil, a place that is the result of the first or natural death). This death can kill the body but not the soul. The second death (linked to hell and the lake of fire) referred to in Scripture can destroy both the soul and the body (Matthew 10:28).

Scripture states that Jesus Christ descended into Hades (*Sheol* in Hebrew) after his death but that death could not hold him. Death had to release him. When this happened, the Devil's jail broke and all of the true believers in him, who had had faith in God from the beginning and were his, were freed by him, and he took them and ascended on high (Ephesians 4:8-10). Now Jesus has the keys to Hades and death because he overcame and took them from Satan (Revelation 1:18).

Since that time, if anyone dies who belongs to the Lord, they do not go to Hades (wrongly translated in most English Bibles as "hell," which really refers to the second death, which is also called the lake of fire). They go to be with the Lord in heaven. This is part of the great victory that he won. In the vision of John in the book of Revelation, the souls of those who have died in the Lord are under the heavenly altar. They are covered by the blood of Christ (and the life is in the blood). They are in the presence of God (Revelation 6:9).

Scripture speaks of a great cloud of witnesses who are aware of what is going on with us, those who are already with the Lord. We also know that Hades or Sheol is full of many unbelievers who are held there, awaiting the general resurrection and the final judgment (Revelation 20:11-15). It is only after that great judgment that the option exists for some to be thrown into the lake of fire (prepared for the Devil and his angels and for all those who follow them and love the lie), which is the second death, the real hell (Revelation 21:8).

Scripture states that all those who are impure seek darkness and uncleanness instead of light and purity (John 3:19-21). The only place we may find light and purity is in the life of the Lord. He gave his life for us so he might offer us life and that we might be saved by his life (Romans 5:10).

The law of life in Christ Jesus comes with a change of life. It is necessary that the life of God must come forth in us. We must be born again (John 3:3-7). Being born the first time from our mother's womb is not sufficient to save us. We can begin to learn many things, but we must be born again by the Spirit of God. Jesus did not tell Nicodemus, who was a great religious leader, that this is optional. He said, *Ye must be born again* (John 3:7).

John relates that this is by water and by Spirit (John 3:5). Spirit relates to life and the life is in the blood (Leviticus 17:11; 1 John 5:6-8). Water symbolizes the Word of God and blood symbolizes the life of God. The Lord desires to plant his Word in us and his living Word will become life unto us. He desires to live and reign in us. He desires to dominate our being. He desires to change us from the inside, to change our very nature, replacing it with his nature until we become servants of righteousness (Romans 6:17-20).

Just as the ring had been upon the finger of Haman, now the ring will be upon the finger of Mordecai. In order for this change to take place, for this double redemption to happen, the role of a clean people of God represented by Queen Esther is essential.

The Lord Jesus is a witness, but the clean people of God are another witness. Two witnesses are required in order to condemn the Devil, the old man, and all those who insist on following the Devil (Numbers 35:30; Deuteronomy 17:6). Notice how this continues in verse 9:

> 9 Then the king's scribes were called at that time in the third month, that is, the month Sivan, on the twenty-third day thereof; and it was written according to all that Mordecai commanded unto the Jews and to the lieutenants and the captains and the princes of the provinces which are from India unto Ethiopia, one hundred and twenty-seven provinces, unto each province according to the writing thereof, and unto each people after their language, and to the Jews according to their writing, and according to their language.
>
> 10 And he wrote in King Ahasuerus's name and sealed it with the king's ring and sent letters by posts on horseback, and riders on mules, mules that were born of mares,

This took place on the twenty-third day of the third month. If we compare this with the calendar of God, the Passover occurs in the first month. That which God ordained to be the source of new life was profaned by man and converted into a problem and into the first law of sin and death.

Haman's first law or decree went forth on the thirteenth day of the first month. The Jewish Passover is on the fourteenth day of the first month; therefore, this first law went into effect starting on the fourteenth day.

Things began to change according to the Jewish calendar on the feast of Pentecost, which came fifty days later (this is when the disciples received power from on high through the infilling of the Holy Spirit). They had to count seven Sabbath days from the Passover and then Pentecost was the day after (always on a Sunday).

Pentecost plays an important part in all of this. The Lord sends his Spirit with his gifts on Pentecost. In the book of Esther, this is similar to the time when Esther is quickened and makes the decision to risk her life to do what she can for her people. This sets a chain of events into motion until Haman is hanged on his own gallows on the twenty-second day of the third month. The Hebrew word used here for *gallows* is the same word that they would have used to refer to a cross or to a large beam of wood (which was used to kill Jesus).

The gifts and ministries of God given by the Holy Spirit are for the express purpose of putting to death the old man (the old nature) even though many do not believe this. Some attempt to use the gifts of the Spirit for personal gain and therefore stimulate the old man. When King Saul attempted this, the true Holy Spirit left him and an evil spirit sent by the Lord troubled him (1 Samuel 16:14).

This caused Saul to hurl his spear at David on repeated occasions. Religious people who yield to demon spirits that are passing themselves off as angels of light think that it would be wonderful to hang "Mordecai" on their gallows. They fantasize that this is what ought to happen to all the true people of God that they perceive as such a hindrance to their plans and program. They become obsessed with getting rid of Mordecai and all who are like him.

When man organizes religion, he begins to contaminate it. He begins to consent to the old man instead of being willing to sacrifice his own life upon the altar of God, so the new man in Christ may come forth. The old man pollutes the worship of God by contaminating it with humanism, which soon turns into the worship of man (the worship of Haman).

Relating Esther to Today

The book of Esther has a historic aspect, but it also refers to us and the present state of the church and the world around us. This will come to a head and to a conclusion at the end of the church age, which is upon us.

At this historic crossroads, many think the Enemy will win. The law of humanism is being circulated far and wide. Shushan (symbolic of the church) has been taken over by "Haman," and the effects of this are seen all over the "127 provinces of the world." School prayer has been prohibited, abortion (even late-term) is legalized, gay marriage is being legalized, and the humanistic agenda has permeated politics, the business world, the media, and the education system. The Enemy has written his law and most of God's people fear this will prevail until the true people of God are extinguished or raptured.

Some of those who believe this have invented a happy end to their problem by teaching that the believers will all be raptured before what they call the great tribulation occurs. They will miraculously be taken away to be with God while the Enemy overruns and controls everything here on earth. This is not the truth. The word *tribulation* is used fifty-five times in Scripture, with most of it being applied to the trials and tribulations that all of God's people are prone to suffer in the world that is under the control of Satan (Haman). What some theologians are calling the great tribulation (described in Revelation 7-19) is really the direct intervention of God as he destroys the wicked sons of the Evil One and removes them from among the righteous. All the sons of God are sealed first, so nothing will happen to them (Revelation 7:3). Jesus said that when we see these things begin to happen, we should lift up our heads (Luke 21:28).

Who do they think has been virtually controlling the world for the last six thousand years? Jesus said Satan has a divided kingdom, and a kingdom that is divided cannot stand (Luke 11:17). The beast of Revelation that represents Satan's kingdom is a seven-headed monster (seven heads is the complete number of many heads over all the kingdoms of this world). Even if he becomes incarnate on earth, Satan will never be able to consolidate his kingdom because it runs on fear and terror instead of on love and trust (like God's kingdom). Satan is in the process of making one last attempt, but like Haman he will fail.

Satan has laced many prevailing church doctrines with lies, so God's people will not be willing to take a stand and risk their lives like Queen Esther. My father taught me, "Our doctrines cannot save us even if they are true; make no mistake, only the Lord Jesus Christ can save us."

Repeating prayers, participating in religious rites or rituals, or believing historical facts or doctrines cannot save us. We must be born again by the Spirit of God and maintain a personal relationship with God by submitting to his correction and discipline. The only way to accomplish this is by coming under the government and authority of the Lord Jesus Christ. This is the place of our eternal security.

The Lord will have an overcoming people who will face the present and the future with unwavering faith. They will not seek to save their own lives. They will be willing to lay down their lives so the life of Jesus might come forth in them. This is certain.

We are entering a time when interesting things will happen. In fact, they are already happening. Over the past centuries and decades, the Enemy has made many attempts to consolidate his power by force, corrupt politics, and manipulation of the economy. It has all failed to bring about a one-world government. The best he can do is the seven-headed monster depicted in Revelation 13. Now, at the time of the end, he is making an all-out attempt to bring the world together spiritually, and is lulling the complacent asleep with smooth words of false peace, while the world is hurtling toward destruction and disaster.

Throughout history there have been many like Mordecai

who have not been in agreement with what the "king" has been doing. They have not been in agreement with where the free will of mankind has led the human race. Those who have been using their freedom to seek personal gain have managed to place the ring of power upon the finger of Haman. The entire fractured and divided world is now worshipping Haman. They are worshipping man instead of God. Satan's kingdom has always been divided, but Jesus said that it cannot stand. In the prophecy of Daniel 2, the feet of the great image depicting the coming world empires are of clay mixed with iron. This represents the corrupt and fragmented state of the current world democracies that will never come together, being mixed with the hodgepodge of laws that men continue to make as they blindly attempt to effect solutions. This is where the stone cut without hands crashes into the image, destroying all the kingdoms of the world (Daniel 2:31-35; Revelation 11:15).

The Lord has a people who are willing to risk their own lives to invite the king (and even those who are like Judas and Haman) to the banquet of the true Word and life of God. This Word, this banquet that God is offering has been going on for two days (two prophetic one-thousand-year days). This special food and drink has one effect on some but an entirely different effect on others.

The Lord has some who do not understand religious terminology. They may not even know the name of the Lord or the historic facts about Jesus, but they yield to the depths of their conscience. On the inside, they love justice and cleanness and light, even if the religious world appears confusing due to all the bad examples that abound (John 10:16).

When Haman had the ring, Scripture states that the city of Shushan was perplexed; they were not at peace. As soon as the ring was placed upon the finger of Mordecai, the city rejoiced and was glad.

This is something that can happen on a personal level in each and every one of our lives and has been going on during the entire church age (Romans 8). The battle between the old man and the new man has been taking place on the stage of all our lives, but now the age of the church is headed into a grand finale. Each of the two laws will come to their respective conclusions because the end of the age is on the horizon.

The gifts of God are only for a season. The time will come for everyone to see the results of what has been planted in each heart and each life. The wheat and the tares have been growing up together, and it is almost impossible to tell them apart until the time of the harvest. Each one produces its fruit. The tares produce poison, and the wheat produces grain, which may be used for food or for seed.

Scripture indicates that the tares must be harvested and bundled first, so that they may be burned; then the wheat may be harvested and placed in the barn (Matthew 13:30). First Haman is hanged, and then Esther and Mordecai receive power and authority. This is 180 degrees reversed from the secret-rapture theory that has lulled so many Christians into a deep, complacent sleep. Scripture states that when men slept, the Enemy came in unawares (Matthew 13:25).

As we were discussing end-times events, an exuberant friend of mine exclaimed, "I'm going up in the first load!" He sobered up immediately when I explained that the "first load" is when God removes the wicked from among the righteous, the tares from among the wheat (Matthew 13:36-43).

One of the reasons the Devil is still fighting so hard is not because the inheritance being offered to the sons of God is off in some never-never-land reachable only by a rapture. It is because a good part of the inheritance of the sons (and daughters) of God, and thus of the people of God, is currently under the management of the Devil. This is why the fight is so intense. In order for the people of God to enter into their true inheritance, the Devil must lose what he has.

The Jews' Defense

Esther 8

Look at what they wrote in the new law:

> 11 *that the king granted power to the Jews who were in all the cities to gather themselves together and to stand for their life, to destroy, to slay, and to cause to perish any army of the people or province that would assault them, and even their little ones and women, and to take the spoil of them for a prey,*
>
> 12 *upon the same day in all the provinces of the King Ahasuerus, namely, upon the thirteenth day of the twelfth month, which is the month Adar.*
>
> 13 *The copy of the writing which was to be given as law in each province was published unto all people and said that the Jews should be ready against that day to avenge themselves of their enemies.*
>
> 14 *So the posts rode upon mules, they went out on mules, being hastened and pressed on by the king's commandment. And the law was given at Shushan, the palace.*

This law is not about going out and seeking real or perceived enemies. This law is about being able to stand up and defend ourselves against any and all aggression. This is a war fought in righteousness, because anyone with bad intentions against the people of God will be sentenced by their own behavior. What they attempt to do to God's people is what God is going to do to them.

In Revelation 11, God has two witnesses who operate under these very same conditions. Whoever attempts to come against them and cause them damage will suffer the exact same consequences. Their evil intentions will come down upon their own heads (Revelation 11:5).

The second law in the book of Esther is more explicit. The people of God are authorized to defend themselves, and this law enters into effect on the thirteenth day of the twelfth month near the end of the calendar.

It is sad that many have taken this new covenant, this New Testament, and have perverted it by turning it into another old covenant of laws and creeds and works of human self-righteousness, when the new law is totally different.

So this new law was to be preached and published just as the first law had been preached and published. The first law, the law of sin and death, was given unto Moses, and it was preached and published for the entire world by the Jews and by legalistic Christians in the church. Similarly, the second law, the law of life in the Spirit, will also be preached and published everywhere (Revelation 14:6).

> 15 *And Mordecai went out from the presence of the king in royal apparel of blue and white and with a great crown of gold and with a mantel of fine linen and purple; and the city of Shushan rejoiced and was glad.*

White speaks of holiness. Holiness is being available for the exclusive use of the Lord.

Blue speaks of royalty and the life of the Lord.

The *mantel of fine linen* is the righteousness of the saints, and *purple* speaks of a royal priesthood.

The Lord will have a kingdom of priests. The *great crown*

of gold means that Mordecai is covered by the very nature of God and, therefore, has all authority with the mind of Christ.

> 16 *The Jews had light and gladness and joy and honour.*

In our present day, we have a divided Christian church and a divided Jewish nation. The two do not appear to be one and the same. We have many individuals in the natural nation of Israel, along with many in the spiritual entity of the church who are not converted to God. They have the name of God and are using the name of God, but their hearts have not been changed, and they are not moving in the nature of God.

The city of Shushan was very perplexed in observing all of this until they saw that Esther and Mordecai began to reign. Then they all rejoiced and were glad. When this happens, all the true people of God will rejoice and be glad.

> 17 *And in each province and in each city wherever the king's commandment and his decree came, the Jews had joy and gladness, a banquet and a good day. And many of the people of the land became Jews, for the fear of the Jews fell upon them.*

The fear of Mordecai and Queen Esther fell upon the people. Scripture states that the fear of the Lord is the beginning of wisdom.

The true people of God have been persecuted for the past six thousand years, so most of those who have gone along with the status quo of this world have not found it convenient to identify with the people of God.

This is a prophecy that things are going to change. Once Haman has been dealt with, many will suddenly become highly motivated to become "Jews." Those who are lukewarm and undecided will be forced to choose a side, and those who make the wrong choice will be destroyed like Haman.

When Haman had the king's ring, he had authority over the world.

The original text could have been translated: *and many of the peoples of the land became Jews.*

Peoples of the land. Very interesting.

Remember that a true Jew is a person with a circumcised heart (Romans 2:29).

We have had many things happen throughout the age of the church: Many messages have been preached and published; many individuals have overcome; many martyrs have given their lives for the Lord and for the cause of the gospel. However, before the end there will be a clean message given through clean messengers everywhere.

The first law produced fear and could not remove sin or guilt, and there are many who continue to preach like this. If you do not repeat this prayer, if you do not agree with and believe these four points, if you do not go to church, if you do not confess your sins, if you do not go to mass or to communion, if you do not pay your tithe here . . . you will come under a curse, you will go to hell!

But this is not how the Lord Jesus preached. He gave some very grave warnings to those who were judging or condemning the hearts of others. Jesus' message was different:

Blessed are the poor in spirit, for theirs is the kingdom of the heavens.

Blessed are those that mourn, for they shall be comforted.

Blessed are the meek, for they shall inherit the earth.

Blessed are those who hunger and thirst for righteousness, for they shall be satisfied.

Blessed are the merciful, for they shall obtain mercy.

> *Blessed are the pure in heart, for they shall see God.*
>
> *Blessed are the peacemakers, for they shall be called the sons of God.* (Matthew 5:3-9)

This sounded different from what the Pharisees of that day and age were preaching. God will also send forth a message now that is different from what the present-day scribes and Pharisees are preaching.

There is no blessing outside of the life of the Lord. The true Spirit of God will not comfort anyone who does not submit to God as his or her King, who does not mourn the old man (the old nature). Without the Spirit of God, it is impossible to be meek. Esther was meek and received the earth as an inheritance. Yet Esther and Mordecai were only examples in a true story many centuries ago that is prophetic of our present time. Now is when the real fulfillment of this prophecy will take place.

The book of Esther does not directly mention the seventh month, which is the setting for the feast of trumpets, the Day of Atonement (or Reconciliation), and the Feast of Tabernacles, which is the fullness of the harvest. The first chapter, however, flags this context as the setting for the entire book.

The book of Esther adds a feast that is not in the law of Moses, the complete fulfillment of which is on the distant horizon for the people of God. The Jews still celebrate this feast, the days of Purim, on the thirteenth and fourteenth days of the twelfth month, almost five months after the Feast of Tabernacles.

At our present time in history, we are in the midst of the fulfillment of the feast of trumpets. These trumpets represent a clean, clear message that is a final ultimatum. Whoever does not afflict their soul and repent, not in theory but in actual practice (by turning their back on their own life), will not be able to enter into the presence of God. They will be cut off from the people of God (Leviticus 23). This is what happened to Vashti.

The end of the book of Esther points us to an event that will take place in more or less "one thousand years" when the day of the Lord ends. This is when these things will be decided once and for all.

Note that this judgment lasts for two days in Shushan, the capital (symbolic of the church), and only one day in the "provinces." This is very interesting. We are in the time when the second law, the law of life in the Spirit, will be applied according to the manner of God. The first time men interfered with the purposes of God, Vashti and her friends refused to come to the feast, just as many of the first invited guests refused to come to the wedding supper in Jesus' parable (Luke 14:15-24). This time men will not interfere; this time, due to Esther and Mordecai, the decree will go forth everywhere with all the authority of the King.

This gospel of the kingdom of God will be preached in the entire world and then the end shall come (Matthew 24:14).

Those who are now preaching that the church shall be defeated, and those who are preaching that a stained, wrinkled, defeated bride will have to be helicoptered out of the battlefield by a "secret" rapture because she cannot endure the supposed horrors of the coming "great tribulation" have not understood the book of Esther or many other Scriptures.

We are now entering the time when we are beginning to fight according to the way of God. We are entering into the time when the Lord will give us the victory. We are entering into the time when we will be able to face these situations and win. Jesus is not about to whisk us off the battlefield and leave the Enemy to run rampant. No! He is about to return to our aid bringing reinforcements, and we shall be caught up (raptured) to meet him in the air as he returns.

From the beginning, God has always had a faithful remnant that has faced the Enemy without being concerned about losing their own lives. They have won many great victories in the eyes of the Lord.

The Lord, however, is not interested in redeeming only people. He will also redeem the earth. The world will come to an end; the world will be destroyed. The world is a system that was initiated by the Devil and is under his government. This present world is primarily a certain way of doing things and is fatally impregnated with the worship of man. On the other hand, Scripture clearly states that the meek shall inherit the earth (Psalm 37:11; Matthew 5:5).

In the Apocalypse, John did not witness the destruction of planet earth. He saw many plagues and other forms of destruction upon the natural man and upon the systems of this world set in the midst of the old creation. Then, without fully realizing how it happened, he saw a new heaven and a new earth before the presence of the throne of God (Revelation 21:1).

Just as the bride of Adam, in her fallen state, was able to influence Adam to choose her instead of God and Scripture, making it clear that the fall was the result of Adam's sin (Romans 5:14; 1 Timothy 2:14), so there will be another woman, the bride of the second Adam, but she will not allow history to repeat itself.

From Genesis 3, it is prophesied that there will be a woman who will give birth to a seed (Christ) who will crush the head of this serpent.

We do not have time to study about the heirs and legacy of Queen Esther, but Scripture refers to some of this in other books of the Bible, such as in the descriptions of the reconstruction of the city and walls of Jerusalem and the Temple with resources from the royal treasury.

This is all of extreme interest.

Is it not of great interest too that the due date of the two laws is the same?

The law of sin and death and the right of God's people to

defend their lives, families, and possessions both come due on the same day, the thirteenth day of the twelfth month!

And do not forget that the countdown for all of this takes place in the twelfth year of King Ahasuerus.

In Scripture, three stages are demonstrated: Children under the age of twelve are under the law of their mothers (Luke 2:41-42); then they may voluntarily submit to their fathers (parents) for another eighteen years (Luke 2:51-52); and then at age thirty they may receive the fullness of their inheritance from their fathers in life. Levites may begin their ministry at age thirty. The priests are of the tribe of Levi (Numbers 4:46-47).

Scripture implies that something very similar will happen to the body of Christ, which is to become a kingdom of priests, a royal priesthood.

Under the law of Moses, children become accountable at twelve years of age, at which time they must assume certain responsibilities and make a key decision. Today, the Jews continue to hold a public ceremony for adolescent males called a bar mitzvah in which they must publically declare whether or not they wish to follow God.

The Lord Jesus had a most interesting time at the temple at Jerusalem when he was about twelve years of age. This is recorded in Scripture (Luke 2:43-50).

It is likely that the decision of Adam and Eve regarding the Tree of the Knowledge of Good and Evil coincided with them having at least twelve years of existence (and it is almost certain that they were forced out of the garden well before they would have turned thirty). Tragically, they did not choose the Tree of Life, and all of their descendants, save one, have been born spiritually dead.

In order for any of us to return to the presence of God, we must be willing to do what Esther did when she chose the will of God instead of her own life. In case you are wondering what happens to those among the priesthood of all believers who do not allow God unlimited access to be able to work in and through them by his grace, they are described by the word of the Lord to the prophet Ezekiel (Ezekiel 44:10-16).

Esther was very motivated to save her people, but we must also note that the king returned to the way of God because of Esther. Before this, he had been consorting and drinking with Haman until Haman got the king to give him his ring of authority. Then Haman had been very busy using the king's ring to write and seal a law to annihilate all the people of God. Meanwhile, the king seemed oblivious to all of the implications and repercussions of Haman's plans. The king was entirely under Haman's influence and spell until he fell in love with Queen Esther. This king represents all of humankind, who have been created in the image and likeness of God, but who have, starting with Adam, irresponsibly ceded their authority to Haman.

There was no other woman who had the grace that Esther had. There was no other woman who would risk her life like Esther. There was no other woman who could serve a banquet like she could to the king and have it end with the king bending over backwards to obey her righteous commands.

The king even left the first banquet convinced that he must make sure that Haman attended the second banquet in accordance with the petition of Esther!

Haman was practically forced to attend the second banquet, which led directly to his death.

Queen Esther overcame evil with good. She did not even wield a sword. She overcame her enemy by hosting two very elaborate banquets in which Haman was a special invited guest.

After this, the fear of Queen Esther, the fear of Mordecai, the fear of the Jews fell upon the entire world until no one dared challenge her again.

God says that this is what will happen regarding his people.

Right now, in most cases, we are still not allowed to defend ourselves, because many of us are not clean and are still capable of doing injustice in the name of the Lord. The time will come, however, sooner than many expect, when the second law will go into effect in fullness.

Let us pray:

> Lord, we ask for understanding regarding the times in which we are living. May we listen to our conscience instead of getting distracted by circumstances. May we follow your will above all else. May we embrace your preparation and guard our words with discretion until it is your timing to reveal things. Amen.

Chapter 7

Our Defense

This book begins with a woman, with a queen who was not trustworthy. She did not come when the king called her. Not only did she not respond, but she was also doing her own thing and refused to leave it when the time came to celebrate something very important that had all the symbolism of the Feast of Tabernacles.

The Feast of Tabernacles is the great feast of God that comes at the end of the harvest. It symbolizes the time when everything accumulated during the growing season has been harvested. There are things that God has been working on for a very long time that are compared to a typical agricultural year. Some crops such as olive trees have to be taken care of for many years before there can be an abundant harvest.

I know that the Lord is conducting Colombia and the world into a time of spiritual harvest. This is supposed to be a great time of celebration, but there is a woman who is causing a lot of trouble. She is the one who really should be the key to all of the success. This woman is a symbol of much of the church, but the church according to the ways of man is not the church according to the ways of God.

This is a woman who does her own thing and completely ignores her husband. Not only this, but she also invited all the other women to join her; therefore, the king, after receiving counsel, decided to take action. He removed Queen Vashti and replaced her with Queen Esther.

In referring to when God gave the law the first time to Moses, Scripture always says, *And God said*. This is the case in Exodus, Leviticus ("*I have said*"), and Numbers. Deuteronomy, however, was not dictated directly by God. This was the law given the second time as it flowed from the transformed heart of Moses under the inspiration of the Holy Spirit. Key segments of this law are aimed at future kings; spiritually it sets the foundation for a *royal priesthood* (1 Peter 2:9; Revelation 1:6).

Queen Esther is not just a woman who lived two thousand five hundred years ago; she also represents the people of God of our time and into the future. She is the manifestation of a prophecy that God will have a people that he will truly be pleased with and who will receive the fullness of their inheritance in Christ.

Those who claim to be the people of God, who claim to be the bride of Christ, who claim to be the queen, and who are doing everything backwards, will soon lose their position. The Lord will choose those who display the qualifications that he desires.

Humanity has gone crazy, and this is the only way to save the situation. The king had given his ring, which represented his power and the capacity to make laws and give orders, to the person who not only desired to do away with Mordecai but who also intended to eradicate the entire Jewish race just because Mordecai refused to worship him.

Many individuals, men and women of God throughout history, have refused to worship man. They have only worshipped God, and the entire world system has been against them.

The Lord says he will change this and he will do so by using a woman (Genesis 3:15).

In Scripture, a woman can represent a people. This is true in the book of Revelation where a special woman gives birth to a son who is very important (Revelation 12).

We know that in God's plans and purposes our Lord Jesus

is not alone. Scripture states that we can become individual members of the body of Christ, of which the Lord Jesus is the Head. This body of Christ has many members, which is another way of seeing the woman who will be the bride of Christ. This woman will be prepared for a very specific time and will receive what the other woman rejected.

This all happens in a place called *Shushan*, which means "lilies," and lilies are also a biblical symbol of the Holy Place (which represents the church) and of this woman. Humanism in the church put the ring, the power, on the hand of the Enemy who was right in there passing himself off as a magnificent angel of light. Haman was very gifted; he was extremely capable, but he was not of God.

Let us examine the details:

In the first month, the decree of the enemy, Haman, went forth in the name of the king. He cast lots (conducted divination by consulting unclean spirits) to determine the month and the day to not only kill Mordecai at the palace but to also slaughter all the people of God in all 127 provinces of the kingdom throughout the earth.

Hitler also desired to do away with as many Jews as possible in as many countries as possible wherever he had the ability to do so. (He also received instructions by dabbling in the occult.) In this instance, Haman attempted to exterminate all of the Jews in the entire known world. We know that this is also an example that shows what will come to pass at the end of the age of the church, and that we are presently living in this time. Scripture states that in Christ there is no difference between Jew and Gentile. It is also clear that our present Enemy hates Christians just as much as he hates Jews. This Enemy desires to exterminate the people of God, and now the people of God include anyone who repents and believes on the name of the Lord Jesus Christ (Romans 11:17-25; 1 Peter 2:10).

The book of Esther is a prophecy about the end of the church age, and we are presently in the midst of it. The time is near (and in another sense this has been going on with individuals and with select groups throughout history) when this woman will risk her life, seeking to effect a change. When she obtains grace, she will also obtain the will of the King and the death of her Enemy.

How can the first law be undone? It cannot be undone.

So a second law must be signed, sealed, and proclaimed. This new law gives the people of God the authority to defend themselves. This is in the Scriptures from the beginning and is very specific in the New Testament.

The New Testament states that the weapons of our warfare are not carnal (2 Corinthians 10:4). Many believe that the New Testament supports pacifism. It is not a pacifist book. The New Testament declares that we are in a war and have certain weapons at our disposal. Our weapons are different from the weapons that the world around us uses.

Our sword is the truth that comes by the Word of God. The Word of God is not just reading verses from the Bible; it is when the Lord himself, by his Spirit, applies his Word in our hearts until he is able to operate through us.

Scripture speaks of a helmet of salvation and full body armor (not just a breastplate) of righteousness (Ephesians 6:14; 1 Thessalonians 5:8). The word translated as *breastplate* in many Bibles really refers to a special (extremely expensive) suit of chain mail, reserved for the kings, that gave total protection (no arrow could penetrate) all the way from the throat to below the knees. It is a coat of mail and a coat of arms.

Righteousness is not what we think is good; it is what God thinks is good. Righteousness is being what God wants us to be, so we can do what God wants us to do. This is the armor that Queen Esther had. She and Mordecai operated with the weapons and with the tactics of God. This is how they were able to overcome evil with good even though the people of God were all hostages in a foreign land. Presently, all Christians live in a hostile world that is under the control of the Devil (Haman) and Jesus wants us to use his weapons and his tactics so that we may walk in his victory.

The date decided upon by Haman the enemy was the thirteenth day of the twelfth month. These are symbolic numbers that are almost at the end of the year, almost at the end of the season. We are almost at the end of the church age.

The woman who is doing her own thing (refusing to follow the King) is saying no one needs to worry about anything, because when the end comes, everyone that belongs to God will be raptured away to the safety of the presence of God before the Enemy wins the day here on planet earth and consolidates his control into a one-world government.

This is not according to Scripture.

God says: The true people of God will be able to stand firm in the evil day until they are victorious (Ephesians 6:13). God says that the Enemy will never be able to consolidate his control because his kingdom is divided and therefore cannot stand (Mark 3:24).

For the Lord has given a second law, a law given after the law of sin and death that has affected and sentenced everyone. This law of life in Christ Jesus is a law of victory and not of defeat (Romans 8:2). It is a law of life and liberty and not of death (James 1:25; 2:12). This is a law by which the true people of God can defend themselves instead of being finished off by the Enemy.

Everything will take place at the proper time.

The Proper Time

Esther 9

1 *Now in the twelfth month, that is, the month Adar,* *Adar* means "glory" or "glorious."

It will be glorious when the Lord Jesus Christ is revealed. Man, apart from God, is not glorious. He is destitute of the glory of God.

Another way to translate this word *glory* is "clarity."

This is the month when God reveals himself. This is the month when God clears things up and clarifies who he is and who his people are. This is the month when it suddenly becomes very clear who Esther and Mordecai really are.

At the end of the season, the Lord is going to clear everything up. He will reveal who his bride really is, who his people really are, and who the real sons of God are. Mordecai represents the sons of God. Esther represents the corporate people of God, who are made up of many sons. *Sons* in this context does not refer to gender because in Christ there is neither male nor female (Galatians 3:28).

Twelve is a fundamental number regarding God's plans. When he began the nation of Israel he used the twelve sons of Jacob, which became the twelve tribes. When the Lord Jesus began his ministry, he selected the twelve apostles. When Judas failed, the prophecy in the Psalms stated that another should take his place (Psalm 109:8). This led the other disciples to think that they should select some candidates and then cast lots to determine who should fill the vacancy (Acts 1:15-26). However, a bit later, someone was chosen by God who was not even on their list. He was the one God used to write much of the New Testament. I am referring to the apostle Paul.

Paul in Greek is essentially the same name as *Mordecai* in

Hebrew. It means "small." Paul did not lord his position over others. He said, "Follow me as I follow Christ" (Philippians 3:9-14).

1 *on the thirteenth day of the same,*

Thirteen, as we have seen, is another fundamental number in Scripture. When Jesus walked here on earth with the twelve apostles, there were thirteen people total. *Thirteen* has to do with the kingdom of God and therefore with the church, but in a negative sense, it can also symbolize rebellion.

The Deliverance of God's People

There were many women, many candidates, but only one (Esther) was chosen as queen. There are many church groups, many different denominations and sects, many man-made divisions, but the true people of God are those whom God has called and chosen, and they, in turn, have chosen God and have been faithful to his call (Revelation 12:17).

Notice that Esther was not attempting to control anyone. She only desired to deliver her people, the people of God who were scattered over the entire world. The Lord Jesus gave his life for his people, and he will have a bride that shares his nature (his virtue, values and concerns).

> 1 *Now in the twelfth month, that is, the month Adar, on the thirteenth day of the same, when the king's commandment and his law drew near to be put in execution, in the day that the enemies of the Jews hoped to have power over them, it was turned to the contrary; for the Jews took dominion over those that hated them.*

The law will be executed. Both the law of sin and death and the law of life in Jesus have serious future implications.

Like the wheat and the tares, the book of Esther offers the

same example: First Mordecai and Esther are formed and positioned, and then the enemies of the people of God are weeded out from among them.

Today, the enemies of the people of God are motivated by a hatred that is just as intense as that which motivated Haman and his friends, and our present situation has not been resolved (yet).

> 2 *The Jews gathered themselves together in their cities throughout all the provinces of King Ahasuerus, to lay hand on such as sought their hurt; and no one could withstand them, for the fear of them had fallen upon all the peoples.*

Note that it does not say that the fear of God had fallen upon some of the peoples; it says the fear of them fell upon **all** of the peoples. No one had feared Queen Vashti and her friends like this. The fear of the overcoming people of God is different.

> 3 *And all the princes of the provinces and the lieutenants and the captains and officers of the king helped the Jews because the fear of Mordecai fell upon them.*

There was a time when most people did not think highly of Mordecai – when Mordecai was dressed in sackcloth at the king's gate and Haman decided it was not enough just to kill him, but that he must also exterminate the entire Jewish race.

The apostle Paul had to face conditions very similar to those faced by Mordecai. Paul and many Christians who have continued to follow in his footsteps have been ruthlessly hunted down and killed by those who harbor the hatred of Haman. Millions of Christians have been killed throughout history (over seventy million just in the Spanish Inquisition), and today there is more persecution of Christians than ever before.

Where will this end?

It will end in what the Scripture calls the first resurrection (Revelation 20:5).

All those who have gone before, including Paul and millions more from righteous Abel forward, will return with the Lord when he is revealed from heaven. Many are watching this situation to see if "Mordecai's" word will stand. They are watching to see if the Word that God has given by his Spirit through many messengers throughout history (as recorded in the Scriptures) will stand.

The Victory

Paul wrote to the Corinthians about when the last trumpet will sound:

1 Corinthians 15

> 52 *in a moment, in the twinkling of an eye, at the last trumpet, for the trumpet shall sound, and the dead shall be raised without corruption, and we shall be changed.*

When that trumpet sounds, there will be a transformation, and some who are here and alive when this happens will be transformed along with others that the world thinks are long dead. They are not really dead because they are alive and with the Lord. The last trumpet is the seventh trumpet (Revelation 10:7).

The life and love that the Lord has placed inside of us, if we are born again by his Spirit, will not die. If we are born again, the shell or body that we live in may pass away, or someone may kill it, but our soul will continue to live in the spiritual realm, in the realm of heaven with the Lord.

So at Shushan, the palace, they decided to see if Mordecai's word would stand. Remember that at Shushan, there were kings from both realms: from Media (the realm of the earth) and from Persia (the eternal realm).

Many have also been watching through the course of church history to see if the words of the apostle Paul in the New Testament will stand. Everyone, including angels and demons, are looking into this.

On the thirteenth day of the twelfth month when the law was implemented, the fear of Mordecai fell upon everyone. They feared the sons of God; they feared those whom the world did not consider worthy. They feared those whom the world thought were weak and powerless because they observed them at the king's gate dressed in sackcloth; they feared those who would not worship man but worshipped God instead. They feared those who were despised and kicked around by the Haman types for thousands of years (Hebrews 11).

And now the time has come for the fear of Mordecai to fall upon all of the people and peoples of the entire world.

> 4 *For Mordecai was great in the king's house, and his fame went out throughout all the provinces, for this man Mordecai waxed greater and greater.*

Like Mordecai, Paul said that he was the least of the apostles. Jesus said the one who is the smallest and is the servant of all is really the greatest in the kingdom of God.

The Lord Jesus also gave us the following admonition:

Matthew 24

> 42 *Watch therefore, for ye know not what hour your Lord doth come.*
>
> 43 *But know this that if the husband of the house knew in what watch the thief would come, he would watch and would not suffer his house to be broken into.*

> 44 *Therefore be ye also ready; the Son of man is to come in the hour that ye think not.*
>
> 45 *Who then is the faithful and prudent slave, whom his lord has made ruler over his household to give them food in due season?*

Esther was faithfully feeding the king and Haman when the critical moment of revelation came.

> 46 *Blessed is that slave whom his lord when he comes shall find so doing.*
>
> 47 *Verily I say unto you, That he shall make him ruler over all his goods.*
>
> 48 *But and if that evil slave shall say in his heart, My lord delays his coming,*
>
> 49 *and shall begin to smite his fellowslaves and even to eat and drink with the drunken,*
>
> 50 *the lord of that slave shall come in a day when he does not look for him and in an hour that he is not aware of*
>
> 51 *and shall cut him off and appoint him his portion with the hypocrites; there shall be weeping and gnashing of teeth.*

What did Mordecai do? He raised Esther (who represents the people of God, the morning star) who was an orphan. Then she unexpectedly became queen. But to obtain true power and authority, she had to risk her life for the welfare of her people.

Mordecai sat dressed in sackcloth (symbol of grief and repentance) at the king's gate while Haman was busy lording it over everyone and smiting his fellow servants. There is a parallel passage in Luke 12 that also describes what will happen to those who are like Mordecai when the Lord Jesus Christ is revealed.

Luke 12

40 *Be ye therefore ready also; for the Son of man comes at an hour when ye think not.*

41 *Then Peter said unto him, Lord, speakest thou this parable unto us or even to all?*

42 *And the Lord said, Who then is that faithful and wise steward whom his lord shall make ruler over his household to give them their portion of food in due season?*

43 *Blessed is that slave whom his lord when he comes shall find so doing.*

44 *Of a truth I say unto you that he will make him ruler over all that he has.*

CHAPTER 8

Destruction and Victory

Esther 9

5 Thus the Jews smote all their enemies with the stroke of the sword and slaughter and destruction and did what they would unto those that hated them.

There has never been a complete fulfillment of this prophecy. The book of Esther is an incredible book because *all* the Jews are saved, and *all* their enemies are defeated until everything goes according to the drumbeat of Mordecai and Esther. This had a direct influence on the return of the people of God to Jerusalem to rebuild the temple and the city and the wall. This is symbolic of what God desires to do now at the end of the church age.

The Lord has a bride in preparation and in training. While she is still immature, she is not able to give many orders, but God has put the crown of the kingdom upon her head (her head is Jesus Christ) and will soon cause her to reign over the entire world. Esther has convinced the "king" to take the signet ring of authority that our forefather, Adam, forfeited many years ago, away from Haman and put it on the finger of Mordecai. Specific individuals will have specific authority.

6 And in Shushan, the palace, the Jews slew and destroyed five hundred men.

Five hundred is a number associated with the throne of God and true worship of God. This includes dealing with anything that is anathema (Leviticus 27:29), such as the Amalekites (the ancestors of Haman the Agagite) that Saul spared when he blatantly disobeyed God (1 Samuel 15:1-23).

These were the henchmen of Haman who had been forcefully fomenting the cult of the worship of man instead of the worship of God. They, like Haman, had been attempting to deify man. When Mordecai refused to worship Haman, and when Haman decided to kill all the Jews, these were the men who would have carried out Haman's evil orders. They were all given a dose of their own medicine.

This is what happens with those who attack or who desire to attack the true representatives of God. What they are planning to do to the people of God will come back upon their own heads.

In the book of Esther, the Jews did not invent the punishment for their enemies. The enemies had decided to exterminate God's people, but God worked it out so that everything became inverted. The second law went forth with the same seal and with the same authority as the first law.

> 7 *Then they also slew Parshandatha, Dalphon, Aspatha,*
>
> 8 *Poratha, Adalia, Aridatha,*
>
> 9 *Parmashta, Arisai, Aridai, and Vajezatha,*
>
> 10 *the ten sons of Haman, the son of Hammedatha; the enemy of the Jews, they slew, but on the spoil they did not lay their hand.*

In this story, Haman represents the Devil and here the Devil has ten sons. *Ten* is the number that has to do with the law. The Devil has been behind the law of sin and death from the beginning. He was the one who beguiled Eve and tempted Adam so they would sin and become subject to death and forfeit the authority (the ring) that God had given them over all of creation. The Devil trapped Adam and Eve and the entire human race in the law of sin and death. Now, as God reverses the Devil's evil plan, destruction suddenly comes upon the sons of the Devil.

It is in the twelfth month that the ten sons of Haman are hanged. Haman was hanged on the twentieth or twenty-first day of the third month.

The real defeat of the Devil was at the cross, but it is at the end of the year (at the end of the age) when the sons of the Devil and the law that he has used so effectively will be defeated for good.

At the time of the end, no one was able to put the first law into effect against the Jews. No one was able to kill any Jews. First of all, if we are truly born again by the Spirit of God, no one can kill the Spirit of God. Second, if our old man that we received from Adam is reckoned dead, if we are dead in Christ, and if we are dead to sin, then no one can bring any charges against a dead person, because the maximum penalty under the law of sin and death is death. So the fear of the Jews became dominant. The fear of Esther and Mordecai became the primary motivating factor for the vast majority of the population.

The doctrine that this world will end with complete domination of evil is completely false. This world system will be brought to an end by the sons of God who will stand firm and victorious on the battlefield to implement the will of God as God directly intervenes in the affairs of men (Ephesians 6:13).

The book of Revelation ends with the fullness of the presence of God here upon the earth, with the veil (heavens) opened, and no more division or separation between heaven and earth. The fullness of God dwells in and among his people and there are new heavens and a new earth.

Because the fullness of God will also be revealed in some of his people (for the body of Christ now consists of many members and Jesus is the Head), we are slow to see many of the parallels between the story of Esther and Mordecai and what is about to take place in our own time in history at the end of the age of the church.

It is that "Vashti," the deposed queen, has the story backwards. She is promising carnal, superficial Christians that they will all go to heaven and relax in mansions, when even the heavens that now exist must be changed and transformed. They will not endure, for there will be new heavens and a new earth. Do you know what will happen now in the heavens? Do you realize that those who are presently in the heavens are preparing for war? They are not just sitting there on nice little clouds playing their harps.

If we carefully read the book of Revelation, it says there will be war in heaven (Revelation 12:7-12). This war will apparently leave the heavens so damaged and in such terrible condition that they must be replaced!

When Jesus came the first time, Scripture says his coming shook the earth. The events relating to his second coming will shake both the heavens and the earth:

Isaiah 34

> 4 *And all the host of the heavens shall be dissolved, and the heavens shall be rolled together as a scroll; and all their host shall fall down as the leaf falls off from the vine and as the leaf falls from the fig tree.*

Isaiah 51

> 6 *Lift up your eyes to the heavens, and look upon the earth beneath; for the heavens shall vanish away like smoke, and the earth shall wax old like a garment, and those that dwell therein shall perish in*

like manner; but my saving health shall be for ever, and my righteousness shall never perish.

2 Peter 3

10 *But the day of the Lord will come as a thief in the night, in which the heavens shall pass away with a great noise, and the elements, burning, shall be dissolved, and the earth and the works that are in it shall be burned up.*

11 *Seeing then that all these things shall be dissolved, what manner of persons ought ye to be in all holy conversation and godliness,*

12 *waiting for and desiring earnestly for the coming of the day of God, in which the heavens being on fire shall be dissolved, and the elements shall melt with fervent heat?*

13 *Nevertheless we, according to his promises, wait for new heavens and a new earth, in which dwells righteousness.*

In light of this,

Hebrews 12

25 *See that you do not refuse him that speaks. For if those who refused him that spoke on earth did not escape, much less shall we escape, if we turn away from him that speaks from the heavens,*

26 *whose voice then shook the earth; but now he has promised, saying, Yet even once, I shall shake not the earth only, but also the heaven.*

27 *And this word, Yet even once, signifies the*

removing of those things that are shaken, as of things that are made, that those things which cannot be shaken may remain.

28 Therefore, receiving a kingdom which cannot be moved, let us hold fast to the grace, by which we serve God, pleasing him with reverence and godly fear:

29 for our God is a consuming fire.

Those who think that they are in for a nice little retirement in heaven playing harps are similar to some who desire to move to Jerusalem. They do not understand what will take place. They may say, "Oh, we want to live in Jerusalem because it is in the Holy Land!"

Do you know what is going to happen in Jerusalem (in the natural land of Israel and also in the worldwide lukewarm church)?

Do you know what the Scripture states will soon happen in Jerusalem as the day of the Lord dawns at the end of the church age?

Zechariah 14

1 Behold, the day of the LORD comes, and thy spoil shall be divided in the midst of thee.

2 For I will gather all the Gentiles against Jerusalem in battle, and the city shall be taken, and the houses rifled, and the women ravished; and half the city shall go forth in captivity, but the remnant of the people shall not be cut off from the city.

3 Then the LORD shall go forth and fight against those Gentiles as when he fought in the day of battle.

Jerusalem (along with the lukewarm church) is entering into another set of serious problems. In fact, it has never been a site of enduring peace and tranquility. Jerusalem has always been surrounded with conflict except for a few years under David and Solomon when God was showing forth examples of things to come.

Scripture clearly states that if God is our Father, we are the sons of a heavenly mother; the heavenly Jerusalem is the mother of us all.

For if we have been born only of a certain group or sect here upon the earth, we could be running the risk that we are not really his, even if the name of Christ has been invoked.

Many people have an earthly church or congregation as their mother, yet God is not their father. If God is truly our Father, then our mother is the heavenly Jerusalem, the city that will descend from heaven and that is described in the final chapters of the book of Revelation.

Chapter 9

The End of Haman's Sons

Esther 9

In order for Jerusalem and the church (the people of God) to be at peace, the ten sons of Haman (the Devil) must be finished off. They must be killed. Their names are significant here. Remember that Jesus did not call the prostitutes and publicans "sons of the Devil." He reserved that title for the scribes, Pharisees, and priests of the contaminated religious order (John 8:44).

The first son of Haman to be slain is *Parshandatha*, meaning "given by prayer." In false religion, everything is given by prayer; everything is based on miracles in the supernatural, beginning with the golden calf.

Moses had gone up the mountain because the people had not wanted to continue to hear the voice of God. They thought that if they did so, they would die (Deuteronomy 5:25). They had sent for God's commandments and had broken most of them before Moses could even return to their camp with the stone tablets. When Aaron offered an explanation to Moses, it was priceless. In essence he said, "We threw our gold into the fire and this calf came out." So what could they do but worship it. A miracle! (Exodus 32:24).

When the natural man prays for what he wants, he can wind up praying to the god of this world, not to the God who is the Creator of the heavens and the earth. The god of this world loves to respond in a "miraculous" manner with a heavy dose of deception. Every pagan shrine has a similar story, and much of this has infiltrated large sectors of the church.

Parshandatha was the first son of Haman to be hanged. Jesus said that when we pray, we should go into our room alone, and our prayer should be private between God and us. Jesus cautioned us against the vain and public repetitions of the religious hypocrites (Matthew 6:5-7).

I have been in many places where well-meaning people pray and pray and pray, yet there is still a lot of disorder in their midst. Their children and young people are rebellious and out of control, while the elders continue their endless prayer meetings in the midst of supernatural manifestations. The same things are repeated over and over with emphasis on volume and on religious cliché. Like the prophets of Baal, they sacrifice themselves until they are bleeding all over (1 Kings 18:26-29).

All of this must be hung on the gallows. This gallows is *fifty* cubits high, which is the number of Pentecost. The true purpose of the gift of the Holy Spirit at Pentecost was to kill off the old man, the old nature, and all of his works (Romans 8:13). The false religion attempts to use the gifts of the Spirit to cater to the whims of the flesh and ends up with a supernatural spirit that is not holy.

The next son is *Dalphon*, whose name means "drip by drip." His father, Haman the magnificent, promises heaven and earth to everyone, but he is unable to deliver. The best he can do is drip by drip in his religion that he has purposely contaminated with the worship of man. If you continue to worship him and to give him your money, he promises that "God" (the god of this world, not the true God) will give you a fabulous return on your investment here and now. The deluded followers continue into more and more deception. For every dollar you give him,

Dalphon will promise you many more in return, but it comes only drip by drip.

Who else must be hung on the gallows of Pentecost?

The third son of Haman is *Aspatha*. His name means "those who are seduced and confined." What does Aspatha do with the people? He seduces them and confines them into a sect or congregation.

Haman has ten sons because *ten* is the number of the law, and this law of sin and death is impossible for anyone to fulfill on their own. Anyone who is guilty on even one point is guilty of breaking the entire law. The only one who was able to fulfill the law once and for all was the Lord Jesus Christ, and this is why he is able to issue a new law of life.

The Lord Jesus came to die and to break the power of sin and death so we can also die to sin and to our corrupt past and have new life in him. Now, whosoever is led by the Spirit of God is not under the law (Galatians 5:18).

There is, however, a woman who used to be queen, who represents a false congregation under the control of the sons of Haman (the sons of the Devil) where the law of sin and death still reigns. This is why they were unable to celebrate the Feast of Tabernacles (Esther 1).

What does this false congregation or system contain?

It contains those who have been seduced and confined into a given congregation, sect, or religion where they are maintained under tight control by the use of endless meetings and ritual.

How does Aspatha manage to keep the people confined and congregated? He does this by the use of guilt. The people are required to make promises that are impossible to keep. They must promise to believe all the doctrines, attend the meetings, pay their tithes and offerings, and abstain from sin (or maybe they are simply encouraged to covenant to submit to one another and/or to a given order of government). When they fail, Aspatha is there to counsel and advise endless religious activity, ceremonies, seminars, penitence, etc. in order to keep the people seduced and confined.

Under Aspatha, the people are required to declare where they congregate and who is their pastor or spiritual advisor or covering. Those who are unable to give Aspatha a satisfactory answer are shunned, because it would be fatal to his scheme to mix those who are free with those whom he has confined and enslaved under the law of sin and death. Aspatha declares those who are free in Christ to be heretics, and he, like his father, desires to rid the world of them.

Aspatha hates Scriptures like Psalm 23: *The LORD is my shepherd [pastor]; I shall not want*, because when Aspatha is their shepherd, everyone who has been seduced and confined by a religious demon spirit is filled with the insatiable desires that fuel his false system. Without the true Holy Spirit, those under Aspatha are confined to bondage. They are slaves to sin and death. Aspatha must be hanged on the gallows (cross) of Pentecost that is fifty cubits high.

The death of the old man (of the old nature) is our only defense.

The fourth son of Haman is named *Poratha*, which means "the fruit of destruction." The Lord seeks good fruit. Scripture implies that when the mature fruit in his people meets with his complete approval and liking, he will return for his bride, for his people who are producing the fruit that he longs for (Song of Solomon 6:11-13). When he returns and examines the fruit of the people of God, there are two outcomes. The sons of the Devil will be destroyed because their fruit is evil and harmful to everyone, and the sons of God will enter in to receive the inheritance of the kingdom.

The fruit of the sons of the Devil will end in destruction, even though they are saying, "If you submit to our order, or if you believe our doctrine, if you repeat our prayers, if you go to our meetings, if you pay us your tithes and offering, it will go well with you." This has some truth to it here in our fallen world, which is under the control of the Devil, but it will not go well in the end.

Since they cannot avoid the large amount of Scripture filled with serious warnings, they invent doctrines where those who meet their prescribed litmus tests are guaranteed a place of safety (here or in heaven) while the Devil consolidates his kingdom here on earth. The serious warnings in Scripture (which encompass at least half of its entire content), according to some of them, are just for those (starting with the Jews) who did not repeat the sinner's prayer. Aspatha never gives the people that he has seduced and confined even the slightest clue that there is about to be a war in heaven (Revelation 12:7), that there will be such a serious, all-out, devastating war in heaven so as to warrant the entire heavens being replaced (2 Peter 3:7-10).

The fifth son of Haman who must be hung is named *Adalia*, meaning "I will be lifted up by JAH." *JAH* is the name of God.

Adalia tells those who have been seduced and confined by false religion that he is the one God has lifted up to be in charge. Adalia claims to be the vicar of Christ. The real vicar of Christ, however, is the Holy Spirit, and a fruit of the Holy Spirit is humility. The Holy Spirit works in those who, like Esther and Mordecai, are humble.

Adalia will be hung on the gallows that is fifty cubits high.

The sixth son of Haman is named *Aridatha*, which means "the lion of the decree." What is the decree? The law of sin and death.

When the book of Esther was written, Satan held the keys to death and the grave. He had sons like Aridatha who were "the lion[s] of the decree."

Things have changed, however. Jesus took captivity captive

and ascended on high. Jesus freed all who were his who were being held by death in the prison of the Devil and ascended on high (Ephesians 4:8-10). Jesus even received the keys (Revelation 1:18).

Satan will be chained for one thousand years in what had been his own prison (Revelation 20:1-3), and Aridatha is headed for the gallows.

Parmashta is the seventh son of Haman. *Parmashta* means "superior." Haman has set up networks of superior brethren who manage everything. They have divided the people of God into categories such as clergy (or five-fold ministry) and laity, instead of the God-ordained priesthood of all believers. This has been going on since ancient times. When Jesus came two thousand years ago, these "superior" brethren were unable to recognize him. In fact, they decided to kill him. Jesus said they had turned his Father's house (which was to be a house of prayer) into a den of thieves (Luke 19:46).

The second time Jesus cleaned out the temple and overturned the tables of the moneychangers, these "superior" brethren condemned him to death. Today, there are still many places claiming to be the house of the Lord, which are really nothing more than dens of thieves under the rule of Parmashta.

The eighth son of Haman is named *Arisai*, which means "the lion of my standards." The emblem on the standard or flag of Haman's son is the lion. The Romans killed almost seven million Christians and fed many of them to the lions at the Coliseum. Christian Rome killed more than seventy million Christians in the Spanish Inquisition alone.

Jesus also has standards, and according to the Song of Solomon, his standard-bearer is a woman (Song of Solomon 6:4, 10), a weak woman such as Queen Esther who comes out of the wilderness leaning upon her beloved (Song of Solomon 8:5).

The ninth son of Haman is *Aridai*, which means "the lion

is sufficient." Jesus started his ministry as the Lamb of God, slain from before the foundation of the world. He said his sheep know his voice and will not follow the voice of a stranger. Jesus is also the lion of the tribe of Judah. If we desire to reign with him, however, we must first be willing to suffer with him (2 Timothy 2:11-13).

No, the lion is not sufficient. Aridai knows nothing about caring for sheep. Aridai knows nothing about being willing to lay down his life for the sheep. Aridai is nothing but a hireling full of bluster and bluff. Aridai is in the same league with Hophni and Phineas, sons of Eli. Scripture declares that they were sons of Belial, another name for the Devil (1 Samuel 2:12). In the face of danger, the hireling flees, but the true Shepherd is willing to give his life for the sheep (John 10:11-16).

Jesus is qualified to be the Good Shepherd because even before the foundation of the world (before Satan and Adam got us all into trouble), Jesus was willing to give his life to redeem us (Revelation 13:8). When Jesus Christ is revealed as the lion of the tribe of Judah, one of the first things on his agenda will be to hang Aridai.

The tenth and last son of Haman is named *Vajezatha*, meaning "as strong as the wind." The word for *wind* is the same as the word for *spirit*.

Vajezatha has many gifts. He is always attempting to prove how strong he is. He is always speaking of exploits and glory. In his massive meetings and concerts, people find angel feathers, gold dust, or other rare, supernatural phenomena. He mentions Jesus but he acts like a rock star.

The time is soon coming, however, when all of this is going to be hung on a gallows that is fifty cubits high. The true Spirit of God, which came at Pentecost, has one primary purpose: to do away with the old man. This is the purpose of the cross.

The word translated *gallows* in Hebrew could have also been translated as *cross*. It simply means a large beam of wood.

The only thing that can end the law of sin is death, and all the sons of Haman are subject to this law. The Scripture does not say the carnal body that sins shall die; it says the soul that sins shall die (Ezekiel 18).

The first death can kill the body but not the soul. There is, however, a second death, a lake of fire called hell, mentioned in Scripture, that can destroy both the body and the soul (Matthew 10:28). This is eternal perdition or destruction (2 Thessalonians 1:9).

Notice in the following passage that the sons of Haman are slain; then Esther pronounces another sentence after this, and they are hanged on the gallows.

For it is appointed unto men once to die and then the judgment (Hebrews 9:27).

> 7 *Then they also slew Parshandatha, Dalphon, Aspatha,*
>
> 8 *Poratha, Adalia, Aridatha,*
>
> 9 *Parmashta, Arisai, Aridai, and Vajezatha,*
>
> 10 *the ten sons of Haman, the son of Hammedatha; the enemy of the Jews, they slew, but on the spoil they did not lay their hand.*

Notice that the Jews were not interested in taking or even touching any of the ill-gotten gains of the sons of Haman.

> 11 *On the same day the number of those that were slain in Shushan, the palace, was brought before the king.*
>
> 12 *And the king said unto Esther, the queen, The Jews have slain and destroyed five hundred men in Shushan, the palace, and the ten sons of Haman;*

> what have they done in the rest of the king's provinces? Now what is thy petition, and it shall be granted thee? What is thy request further, and it shall be done?
>
> 13 Then said Esther, If it please the king, let it be granted to the Jews who are in Shushan to do tomorrow also according unto this day's decree, and let Haman's ten sons be hanged upon the gallows [Hebrew *stake*].

Notice that Esther passes judgment a second time on the sons of Haman after they were already slain in verses 7-10; she requested that they be hanged upon the gallows.

The Final Judgment

> 12 And the king said unto Esther, . . . Now what is thy petition, and it shall be granted thee? What is thy request further, and it shall be done?

What do you really want, Queen Esther? The king has already placed the ring of complete authority of the kingdom onto the hand of Mordecai. He is no longer blathering about fulfilling Esther's petition and request for up to *the half of the kingdom*. The king, for quite some time now, has been willing to place his entire kingdom into the hands of Esther and Mordecai, even though Esther continues to respect the dignity of the king and continues to consult him on all these important matters.

But what does Esther really desire?

> 13 Then said Esther, If it please the king, let it be granted to the Jews who are in Shushan to do tomorrow also according unto this day's decree, and let Haman's ten sons be hanged upon the gallows.
>
> 14 And the king commanded it to be so done; and

> it was given as law at Shushan; and they hanged Haman's ten sons.
>
> 15 And the Jews that were in Shushan gathered themselves together also on the fourteenth day of the month Adar and slew three hundred men at Shushan; but on the spoil they did not lay their hand.

Three is a number linked to fruit and to fruitfulness, and one hundred represents the plan of God; therefore, three hundred means the plan of God is coming to fruition. In the earlier stages of the growing cycle, it may still be possible for an unrighteous person to be turned around (Ezekiel 18). However, once the fruit has come to maturity (remember that the seed is in the fruit), a judgment or determination must be made. If the mature fruit is poisonous, the time for leniency is over, and the Lord and his bride will not forgive this. They cannot, for otherwise the poison will continue to spread.

The tares produce poison. If they are not gathered and burned, it is not safe to allow flocks to pasture in the fields after the harvest. Those who would glean what is left of the wheat would be in danger of being poisoned.

Scripture is clear that everything that bears evil fruit will be burned at the time of judgment.

> 16 And the other Jews that were in the king's provinces also gathered themselves together and stood for their lives and had rest from their enemies and slew of their foes seventy-five thousand, but they did not lay their hands on the spoil,

Those who claim that the sons of God will take over the kingdoms of this world and reign from the White House or from the EU or from the Vatican or from the UN are mistaken.

The true people of God will not lay their hands on any of this "spoil" after the final battle, because the kingdom of God is a completely different system that is incompatible with the corrupt kingdoms of this world. The kingdoms of this world will collapse and fall, and the kingdom of God will replace them and never become corrupted (Daniel 2:44; Revelation 11:15).

> 16 *but they did not lay their hands on the spoil,*
>
> 17 *on the thirteenth day of the month Adar; and on the fourteenth day of the same they rested and made it a day of banquet and gladness.*
>
> 18 *But the Jews that were at Shushan assembled together on the thirteenth day thereof and on the fourteenth thereof; and on the fifteenth day of the same they rested and made it a day of banquet and gladness.*
>
> 19 *Therefore, the Jews of the villages that dwelt in the unwalled towns made the fourteenth day of the month Adar a day of gladness and banquet and a good day and of sending portions one to another.*

This may very well be where the custom of giving gifts to one another in the twelfth month (our December) began.

There were two days of warfare in Shushan, the palace, and only one day of war in the provinces.

We have now had two prophetic days (two thousand years) of warfare in Shushan, which is symbolic in Scripture of the church and the feast of Pentecost. The Feast of Tabernacles (symbol of the fullness of the kingdom) was to have been inaugurated a long time ago, but this did not happen due to Vashti, a woman symbolizing a church or congregation, who deceived herself and many others by her own beauty.

It has taken two days, two thousand years, to straighten out Shushan under the government of Esther, and in the provinces (the world) it will only take one day. This is the famous day of the Lord described by all the prophets, which is coming up on our calendar. For it is only as the Lord is able to straighten out Shushan (the church) that it is possible to preach the fullness of the law of life in Christ Jesus to the rest of the provinces (the world).

Now is the opportune time to do this. Now is the time for God's people all over the world to stand up and fight and defend themselves with the spiritual weapons (starting with the truth) that have been provided for us. Now is the time for the law of the spirit of life in Christ Jesus to be proclaimed in fullness (Romans 8:2).

The Days of Purim

When Vashti was queen and when Haman had the king's ring, Shushan was sad and perplexed. The city did not rejoice until the government was in the hands of Esther and Mordecai.

The city of God will soon rejoice.

> 20 *And Mordecai wrote these things and sent letters unto all the Jews that were in all the provinces of King Ahasuerus, both near and far,*
>
> 21 *to establish this among them that they should keep the fourteenth day of the month Adar and the fifteenth day of the same, yearly,*
>
> 22 *as the days in which the Jews had rest from their enemies and the month which was turned unto them from sorrow to joy and from mourning into a good day, that they should make them days of banquet and joy and of sending portions one to another and gifts to the poor.*
>
> 23 *And the Jews accepting this began to do as Mordecai had written unto them.*
>
> 24 *Because Haman, the son of Hammedatha, the*

Agagite, the enemy of the Jews, had devised against the Jews to destroy them and had cast Pur, that is, the lot, to consume them and to destroy them,

25 but when she came before the king, he commanded by letters that his wicked device, which he devised against the Jews, should return upon his own head and that he and his sons should be hanged on the gallows.

26 Therefore, they called these days Purim after the name of Pur. Therefore, for all the words of this letter and of that which they had seen concerning this matter and which had come to them,

When wicked Haman attempted to wipe out the Jews because Mordecai refused to worship him, he cast lots – or Pur – to determine when to carry out his evil plot. Pur or lots relate to the inheritance (Numbers 33:54).

The Jews had been expelled from their inheritance, and Haman wished to wipe them off the map. Through all of this, the celebration of the days of Purim is born. This is symbolic of entering into the fullness of the inheritance and is added in the book of Esther to the three feasts ordered by God in the law of Moses in Leviticus 23.

27 the Jews ordained and took upon them and upon their seed and upon all such as joined themselves unto them, so as it should not fail, that they would keep these two days according to their writing and according to their appointed time each year,

28 and that these days should be remembered and kept throughout every generation, every family, every province, and every city, and that these days

> *of Purim should not fail from among the Jews nor the memorial of them perish from their seed.*

Many have falsely prophesied that the people of God will all be destroyed unless God takes them out of the world by way of a secret rapture, and that after the church is raptured, everything will seriously degenerate as the Devil consolidates his reign upon the earth.

This book of Esther, however, paints an entirely opposite view. Those who lose are the enemies of the people of God, because at the last minute, God intervenes in a most unexpected way, and God's people receive an official authorization to defend themselves.

The days of Purim are instituted and are symbolic of the fullness of the inheritance. Those who desired an inheritance by attempting to eliminate the people of God were completely destroyed, and God's people came out on top with the reins of power to dominate the world.

> 29 *Then Esther, the queen, the daughter of Abihail, and Mordecai, the Jew, wrote with all authority, to confirm this second letter of Purim.*

In this matter of life and death, Mordecai was the first witness and then Esther wrote to confirm as the second witness.

> 30 *And he sent the letters unto all the Jews, to the hundred twenty-seven provinces of the kingdom of Ahasuerus, with words of peace and truth,*

> 31 *to confirm these days of Purim in their times appointed, according as Mordecai, the Jew, and Esther, the queen, had enjoined them, and as they had decreed for themselves and for their seed, the words of the fastings and their cry.*

> 32 *And the commandment of Esther confirmed these words of Purim, and it was written in the book.*

This is the first time that a woman writes law in the Scripture, and she prefigures the bride of Christ who is the second witness necessary to bring down the entire empire of the Devil.

Greatness of Mordecai

Esther 10

1 *And King Ahasuerus laid tribute upon the land and upon the isles of the sea.*

Here is the fulfillment of Psalm 2. King Ahasuerus is now a type and shadow of the human race back under the perfect government of God. Jesus Christ is the Head, and he will rule the (unconverted) nations with a rod of iron (Revelation 2:27; 12:5; 19:15). Adam walked with God in the garden before the fall, but the presence of God was exterior. Jesus Christ is the Son of Man, but he has the fullness of the presence and nature of God inside, for he is also the Son of God. He is surrounded with brethren operating in the fullness of the Holy Spirit like Mordecai and Esther.

2 *And all the acts of his power and of his might and the declaration of the greatness of Mordecai, unto which the king advanced him, are they not written in the book of the chronicles of the kings of Media and Persia?*

3 *For Mordecai, the Jew, was next unto King Ahasuerus and great among the Jews and accepted of the multitude of his brethren, seeking the good of his people and speaking peace unto all his seed.*

The Lord will soon cause his true sons to reign. The battle has lasted for two days (two thousand years) in Shushan (in the realm of the church). Now the war will be waged in all the "provinces" throughout the world, for we are entering the day of the provinces, the day of the towns and villages without walls.

Ezekiel prophesied regarding this day and the evil intentions of the Enemy of the people of God (Ezekiel 38). The Enemy will make another attempt to destroy God's people, but his plans shall become inverted. The evil that he has planned to bring upon the people of God shall come down upon his own head.

This is what Ezekiel prophesied, what Isaiah saw, and what John records in the book of Revelation. This is also recorded in the Song of Solomon and in virtually every book in the Bible referring to it in one way or another.

The sons of Haman (the sons of the Devil) and all that they represent will be slain and judged. The law of sin and death will come undone when everything is fulfilled (Matthew 5:18), and the love and life of the Lord Jesus Christ will reign in and through a special people that he has joined to himself. This is the prophecy of Esther.

Proverbs 4

18 But the path of the just is as the light of the morning star, that shines more and more until the day is perfect.

Let us pray:

Lord, thank you for your clarity, for your glory. We ask that we might see these things with ever-greater clarity and not give up in the face of increasing adversity as your special day looms on our horizon. May all the enemies of your people be defeated and apprehended. May none of them escape. We ask this in the name of our Lord Jesus. Amen.

Conclusion

The real fulfillment of the prophecies of Daniel and Esther and Zechariah are for us. We are entering the time of fullness and judgment. Some will enter in and others will be cut off. The fact that God has unsealed this message means that the time of fulfillment is upon us. The realm of the Holy of Holies is before us.

In 1983, I was captured and held hostage for five months, starting on August 14, by FARC rebel guerrillas who tied me to a tree in the jungle. On the dates of the feast of trumpets, I had a supernatural visitation from the Lord that included a ringside seat to witness an extremely rare astronomical event involving Venus, the morning star, as related in my book *Rescue the Captors*. After that, the Lord led me on a 100-day Bible study in which he opened up my understanding in relation to all the books of the Bible. Two days later, I was miraculously released and was launched into a worldwide ministry that has gradually intensified over the past thirty-one years.

The Lord showed me that 1967 (I was twelve years old at the time) was the 69th Jubilee since the writing of the book of Leviticus circa 1883 BC; therefore, 2017 will be the 70th Jubilee, and I believe it will prove to be a significant prophetic event (Ezekiel 46:16-18). The year 1967 was when the Six-Day War happened in Israel, and the Jews regained Jerusalem. It was also the year many key ministries began, including Voice of the Martyrs and all ministries that came forth from the "Jesus People," as many hippies on the university campuses came to Jesus Christ.

I expect that 2017 will be much more intense. We are presently in a sequence of four blood moons alternating between Passover and Tabernacles on Jewish feast days, with the last one occurring on September 28, 2015, which is the date of the Feast of Tabernacles. The Jewish New Year on the 13th of September marks the beginning of the forty-ninth year (the seventh seven) of the Jubilee cycle. The fall of 2016 will be the beginning of the fiftieth year. The four blood moons are a sign of impending judgment upon Israel and upon the realm of the church.

Many are expecting serious judgment to first be poured out upon America and upon the secular world. This will no doubt eventually happen if the present state of affairs continues. However, I have a different view. I see that according to Scripture the judgment starts from the house of the Lord. Those who are misrepresenting God in Israel and in the worldwide church will be first in line when God begins to separate the wicked from the righteous. When God's people are clean, the secular world will have a golden opportunity to repent and come to Jesus Christ.

Daniel 9

24 *Seventy weeks are determined* [Hebrew *cut*]

When Abraham made a covenant with God, Scripture says he *cut* a covenant, and the sign of that covenant was circumcision (Romans 4:11). When God enters into a covenant with us, he is going to cut. In order for us to be brought into compliance in a covenant with God, he must cut out of us what he does not like. This is called circumcision of the heart (Romans 2:29).

24 *Seventy weeks are determined* [Hebrew *cut*]

> *upon thy people and upon thy holy city to finish the prevarication and to conclude the sin and to make reconciliation for iniquity and to bring in everlasting righteousness and seal the vision and the prophecy, and to anoint the Holy of Holies.*

If you take this on a year-for-a-day basis, this is prophesying the first coming of Jesus Christ, and Jesus was literally cut off in the last week of the prophecy. But weeks in the Bible are sometimes equivalent to generations. From Adam to Christ are seventy generations, and this prophecy is fulfilled in the generation of the Christ, in which we still exist. The generation of the Christ has not concluded, for now the body of Christ has many members and Jesus is the Head. But for some of us who are alive and remain, it is yet to be determined who is in and who is out in terms of who will reign and rule with Christ for one thousand years. I know there are many ways to look at this, but Paul indicated that he was pressing on to the mark for the prize of the high calling, and I tend to relate this to the first resurrection (Philippians 3:14; Revelation 20:4-5).

And it may be that many people will be saved in a certain sense but excluded from the generation of the Christ, because the generation of the Christ, the royal priesthood, is exclusive to those who will reign and rule (1 Peter 2:9). If you add up the forty-two generations (fourteen times three) mentioned in Matthew 1:17 (from David to Christ), Jesus is the forty-first, and the many-membered body of Christ is the forty-second. This includes all the members of the bride of Christ without spot or wrinkle or any such thing. Christ is the end of all genealogies in the Bible, and the generation of Christ continues today. This is the generation that will remain until all things mentioned in Matthew 24, Mark 13, and Luke 21 are accomplished (Matthew 24:34; Mark 13:30; Luke 21:32).

We cannot even be 100-percent sure of what is going to happen to someone like Judas in the final judgment, because God is the ultimate judge. We know for certain from Scripture that Judas lost his place. He irrevocably lost his place as an apostle, even though it appeared that he made an attempt at repentance between the death and the resurrection of the Lord (Matthew 27:3-4). But he never made it to the resurrection because he had already gone past the point of no return. This is similar to what happened with wicked Haman when he pleaded with Queen Esther after he had been found out, but it was too late.

Some people think that the prophecy of Daniel 9 was fulfilled with the first coming of the Lord with his death and resurrection. Yet it was not completely fulfilled.

Listen to this:

> 24 *to finish the prevarication*

Prevarication is old English and comes from a root that means to twist things and to use them for a purpose that they were not designed for. So when we take the talents that God has given us and use them for our own means, to get something for ourselves, that is what we are doing. We are using our God-given gifts for something they were not designed for.

Holiness is not a way of talking or a way of dressing or religious rites and rituals. Holiness means being separated for the exclusive use of the Lord. That means being available exclusively to the Lord for whatever he wants from us.

> 24 *to conclude the sin*

The existence of sin in the lives of the people of God is not concluded right now (although full provision has been made at the cross) as long as the old man, the old nature, is still alive. Scripture states that it is appointed unto men to die once, and after this the judgment (Hebrews 9:27). It is a good start for us to reckon the old man dead with Christ when we receive the gospel, but God has this wired. The only way out of the natural realm that we live in is to die, for flesh and blood cannot inherit the kingdom of God (1 Corinthians 15:50). In the next verse, Paul calls this a mystery and links it to the resurrection of the dead. This also presents additional problems for the secret-rapture hypothesis.

24 *and to make reconciliation for iniquity*

Iniquity refers to doing things our own way and covering up and hiding to a point where it looks right but it is not. Iniquity also refers to darkness and hiding something from the light. And reconciliation means straightening out. Reconciliation for iniquity means straightening us out so we are straight and clean and back in the light.

24 *and to bring in everlasting righteousness and seal the vision and the prophecy, and to anoint the Holy of Holies.*

We know that the Holy of Holies is in the realm of the Feast of Tabernacles, which is still ahead of us, because most of the people making up the church (in the priesthood of all believers) are still in the Holy Place of ministry. A veil still separates many of them from the Holy of Holies. And in order to enter into the life of Christ, which is the prerequisite to entering the Holy of Holies, we must come individually, one by one.

But also in the type and shadow of leaving the wilderness and going into the Promised Land, this was not something that Joshua and Caleb and the Israelites could do one by one. It had to be the entire corporate people of God and it had to be done at the time that God prescribed (Joshua 3:17). In the wilderness, Joshua could dwell in the tabernacle (Exodus 33:11), but in order to get into the Promised Land (symbolic of the fullness of our inheritance in Christ), the Israelites had to corporately cross the Jordan River (symbolic of death) and enter. God did, of course, make supernatural provision. Paul calls this a mystery (1 Corinthians 15:51).

One of the terrible problems with a lot of modern Bibles is the change of the pronouns when they take *thee, thy, thou, ye,* and *you* and change them all to *you*. *Thee, thou,* and *thy* (anything that begins with "t") are always singular, and *ye* and *you* in old English are always plural. There are roughly thirty-three thousand promises in the Bible, and some of them are for the corporate people of God that can only be fulfilled corporately, and others are promises that can be taken individually. If you mix that all up by taking the distinction between singular and plural out of the Bible, then people unconsciously think that the corporate promises can be appropriated individually because that is the impression they get from reading their oversimplified Bibles. They lose their heart for the corporate people of God, and some begin to think of themselves as spiritual Lone Rangers.

Jesus summed up the Law and the prophets by saying that we should love the Lord our God with all our heart and all our soul and all our mind, and that we should love our neighbor as much as we love ourselves (Matthew 22:36-40). Queen Esther put this into practice.

If you mistake it the other way, in order to have a corporate people of God who can fulfill the requirements for the corporate promises of God, individuals must be dealt with one by one. Unless we experience some things as individuals, and understand what it is to crucify that old man and bring him down and deal with our own personal situations, we cannot really come to maturity among the wonderful corporate people of God who are going to collectively inherit the kingdom.

So we continue to have people trying to apply things corporately without dealing with the individual issues. Some individuals also try to inherit the corporate promises, but they have absolutely no chance of success.

25 Know therefore and understand that from the going forth of the word to cause the people to return and to build Jerusalem unto the Anointed [Hebrew Messiah] Prince, there shall be seven weeks, and sixty-two weeks,

Seven times seven or forty-nine years after the decree that allowed Ezra and others to return to Jerusalem, there was a shadow fulfillment of the Feast of Tabernacles under Nehemiah with the rebuilt wall and temple. If you add sixty-two weeks times seven (a year for a day), this will take you to the beginning of the ministry of Jesus. This is why some of the disciples were looking for the Messiah at the specified time (John 1:45). The final week with the crucifixion in the middle would have ended about the time the Holy Spirit was poured out upon the household of Cornelius (Acts 10). This was a grand total of 490 years composed of 49 plus 434 plus 7. There were 434 years.

25 while the street shall be built again and the wall, even in troublous times.

26 And after the sixty-two weeks the Anointed One [Hebrew Messiah] shall be killed and shall have nothing: (and the ruling people that shall come shall destroy the city and the sanctuary; whose end shall be as a flood, until at the end of the war it shall be cut off with desolation).

27 In one week (they are now seventy) he shall confirm the covenant by many: and at the midst of the week he shall cause the sacrifice and the oblation to cease, and because of the many abominations, desolation shall come, even until complete destruction shall be poured out upon the abominable people.

Jesus was cut off in the middle of the seventieth week in the midst of his ministry. By AD 67 or so (which should have been the thirty-first Jubilee from the giving of the book of Leviticus circa 1483 BC), the situation had degenerated into the war described by Josephus when Jerusalem was completely destroyed for the second time. Yet it is also clear in Matthew 24, Mark 13, and Luke 21 that the destruction of Jerusalem in AD 66-70 was also a type and shadow of the end of the age of the church, which is now upon us.

But friends, I see another dimension to this prophecy. I see the seventieth generation, the generation of Christ (the seventieth from Adam according to Luke and the forty-second from David according to Matthew), with us coming into a time when we are about to experience the second coming, and this will all be completely resolved for the genuine sons of God. The Scripture that the Lord gave me together with Daniel 9 is Leviticus 23:23-31. The book of Esther gives a clear picture of all of this and how it applies to our present time.

The Day of Reconciliation

The first twenty-two verses of Leviticus 23 describe the Feast of Passover (historically linked to the fifteen-hundred-year age of the law and the Jews) and the feast of Pentecost (historically linked to the two-thousand-year age of grace and the church). Spiritually, Passover is linked to salvation and Pentecost is linked to the infilling of the Holy Spirit. Under the law, there were only three required meetings a year for Israel that were called the feasts of the Lord and are described here in Leviticus 23. In the Bible God does not ordain the synagogue system. The Israelites came up with that on their own, and the church in many cases has done them one better.

> 23 *And the LORD spoke unto Moses, saying,*
>
> 24 *Speak unto the sons of Israel, saying, In the*

seventh month in the first day of the month, ye shall have a rest, an alarm for a reminder, and a holy convocation.

The feast of trumpets began in the seventh month on the first day. It marked the beginning of a new moon, which is symbolic of the people of God (Israel and the church) coming into victory. It is also the Jewish New Year on the sacred calendar and was likely the real date of birth of the Lord Jesus Christ. Isaiah prophesies the complete fulfillment of this:

Isaiah 30

26 Moreover the light of the moon shall be as the light of the sun, and the light of the sun shall be sevenfold as the light of seven days, in the day that the LORD binds up the breach of his people and heals the stroke of their wound.

Isaiah 60

20 Thy sun shall set no more; neither shall thy moon wane: for the LORD shall be thine everlasting light, and the days of thy mourning shall be ended.

21 And thy people shall all be righteous; they shall inherit the land for ever; they shall be shoots of my planting, the work of my hands, that I may be glorified.

So when God's people are what God wants them to be, we will not have any more of this waxing and waning in the church. God is going to shine; Jesus is going to shine sevenfold. One of the biggest problems today is in how the world perceives Christians. There is strife and abomination and corruption among people calling themselves by the name of the Lord because of the lack of a clean, corporate people for God to put on display.

In this sense, most of natural Israel and the lukewarm church are both in similar trouble. They are using the name of the Lord and, therefore, are a big target for the Enemy. But if their hearts are not clean, they are unable to overcome. Christians in name only are being slaughtered in many places of the world today, similar to what has happened to many Jews. And yes, many outstanding and true Christians and Jews have also been martyred over the years. However, I see a big change coming as we enter the day of the Lord.

Those who are clean will be sealed (Revelation 7), and anyone who is using the name of the Lord and is not clean or sealed will not only receive the full brunt of the Enemy onslaught but also the judgments of God (some of which may be linked). When God refers to *his people*, he does not dwell on all the manmade factions, denominations, differences, and distinctions in what man calls the church, or even between what some call natural Israel and spiritual Israel. God's people are all those who have been redeemed by the Lord Jesus Christ, and in Christ there is no division between Jew or Greek, or male or female. There is no basis for the salvation of anyone past, present, or future other than the work of redemption of our Lord Jesus Christ.

When the unbelieving Jewish nation was cut off, many believing Jews were not cut off; and when the Gentile believers were grafted in, they were told to not think more of themselves than they ought (Romans 11:17-21). The root of the good olive tree is not the Jewish nation, it is Christ. God even seems to indicate that he will soon bring at least some of them to repentance as a nation and that he is able to graft them back into Christ (Zechariah 12:9-14; Romans 11).

2 Peter 1

19 We have also the most sure word of the prophets,

> unto which ye do well that ye take heed, as unto a
> light that shines in a dark place, until the day dawns
> and the morning star arises in your hearts,

This is essential in order to judge the world.

God will do it. We cannot do it even when we have gifts and ministries and the greatest talents God has given us that we can take and use in our own life. We cannot do it. It has to be him, in his life. He wants to do his work in us, and he wants to do his work through us. His work is the only thing that will stand in the end.

The corporate people represented by Queen Esther (the bride of Christ) are the work of his hands. They include all of the redeemed.

Leviticus gives a continuation of the entrance requirements that God set forth for this very special day, the day of the Lord.

Leviticus 23

> 25 Ye shall do no servile work therein; but ye shall
> offer an offering on fire unto the LORD.

This catches the Hebrew – *an offering on fire.*

Friends, we are the offering. The question is: Are you on fire with the real fire? Because there is strange fire all over the place.

But are we on fire with the real fire of the Lord? It takes the Lord. We are not to be running around playing with matches, lighting off false or strange fire.

> 25 Ye shall do no servile work therein; but ye shall
> offer an offering on fire unto the LORD.

Notice this: It does not address this in the singular. There is a *ye*. This is a message to the corporate people of God.

> 26 *And the LORD spoke unto Moses saying,*

> 27 But the tenth day of this seventh month shall be the day of reconciliations;

Reconciliation in Scripture means lining everything up straight again, like God is straight and true. This is the meaning of the word *reconciliation* as it is defined by God's usage of the term.

> 27 it shall be a holy convocation unto you; and ye shall afflict your souls and offer an offering made on fire unto the LORD.
>
> 28 And ye shall do no work in this same day; for it is a day of reconciliations, to reconcile you before the LORD your God.
>
> 29 For every person that shall not afflict themselves in that same day, shall be cut off from among his people.

Friends, this is a prophecy that applies to us. In order to get to the Feast of Tabernacles you must go through what in some Bibles is called the Day of Atonement. Here it is translated as the *day of reconciliations*.

The word *reconciliation* is an important term in the Bible, but it is not translated accurately in many translations. Beginning in Genesis, God told Noah to build an ark with three levels. Then the Hebrew text does not literally say, "pitch it within and without with pitch." Rather, it says, *reconcile it within and without with ransom*.

Genesis 6

> 14 Make thee an ark of cedar trees; rooms shalt thou make in the ark and shalt reconcile it within and without covering it over with pitch [Hebrew *ransom* or *atonement*].

This is the first usage of the word *reconcile* and the first usage of the word *ransom* that form key patterns throughout the Scriptures. Ransom is what Jesus did for us to redeem us so we could be brought out of darkness and back into the light. This ransom is linked to his blood and the life is in the blood (Leviticus 17:11). The gospel is very clear in the book of Leviticus.

This ransom works because he gave his life for us. Unless we are willing to let go of our own life and let his life come forth in us, we cannot be straightened out. This is repentance and requires the grace of God. This means we must repent and turn from our own works, so his work may be accomplished in and through us. The gospel that some preach of "only believe" is deficient. Jesus said, *Repent ye and believe* (Mark 1:15). When Jesus said *only believe,* it was related to a physical healing (Mark 5:36; Luke 8:50) when Jairus's daughter was resurrected (as Jesus followed up on John the Baptist's ministry that had called the nation to repentance). It is after repentance that we are to believe and place our faith in him, so we depend upon his resurrection life (Romans 5:10). This is why John the Baptist was sent to prepare the way of the Lord (Luke 3:1-18).

Reconciliation in the old English dictionaries is still a shipbuilding term. It means lining everything up straight. If all the planks are lined up straight, the water will not come into the boat. If we are lined up straight with Jesus, together with all of the others who are lined up with him, there will be an "ark" of salvation that has three levels (Genesis 6:16) which will go through the coming judgment intact (Matthew 24:37-39; Luke 17:26-27). The three levels have to do with the three obligatory feasts prescribed by God for Israel and with the three courts of the temple. Scripture defines Scripture when the same thing is always translated the same way, such as in the *Jubilee Bible*.

Reconciliation (being lined up straight with God) is absolutely necessary. There isn't any way into the Feast of Tabernacles without going through the feast of trumpets and the Day of

Reconciliation (which are preludes to the Feast of Tabernacles). This is the fullness of repentance and faith. This is when our faith merges with the faith of Jesus, so we have one faith (Ephesians 4:5). This is where we become one with Jesus, as he is one with the Father (John 17:21).

It is possible to get into the Feast of Passover (salvation) or even the Feast of Pentecost (the infilling of the Holy Spirit) by simply agreeing with God: agreeing to repent and place our faith in Jesus and agreeing to come under the discipline of our heavenly Father as his sons. The Feast of Tabernacles, however, is different. In order to get in, we must be conformed to his will. This is the result of grace and requires our faith to be merged with his into one faith as we come to maturity in the body of Christ.

When William Tyndale translated the word for the top or cover of the ark of the covenant as the *mercy seat,* he made a valiant effort but missed the meaning of the original terminology. The Hebrew literally means "seat of reconciliation," and it is over the ark. This is where the blood (life) is applied – where we can be lined back up and straightened out in the life of Christ. This takes place in the direct presence of God (Zechariah 3:1-5) in the realm of the Holy of Holies.

Anyone attempting to enter into the Holy of Holies without the blood (without the life of Jesus) will be destroyed. The only one who was able to enter properly was Jesus. And the only way for us to enter the presence of God the Father is in his life. It is in the presence of God and in the life of Jesus that all of these promises are "yes" and "amen" in us (2 Corinthians 1:20).

This realm of the church today (linked to the Holy Place, to the Feast of Pentecost and to the earth) is a realm that is fading like an open flower and will be cleansed by fire and merged with the Holy of Holies (2 Peter 3:10). The realm of Pentecost is not a realm that will remain. We know that the fullness of the Feast of Tabernacles for God's people is on the horizon. But first comes the Day of Atonement, the Day of Reconciliation. It is not only a day of God's people coming corporately back into the presence of God (back into the realm of the Holy of Holies), but it is also a day in which those who will not afflict their own souls and will not turn their backs on their own lives will be cut off. This is what happened to Vashti. Those who will not repent from their own works will be destroyed. This is what happened to Haman.

Friends, in Pentecost, the symbolism is still that of a field that was planted with good seed and with tares. Both come up together, but before the end, the tares will be bundled and burned. Then the wheat will be taken into the barn (Matthew 13:24-30).

What We Do Not Tell Sarah

Leviticus 23

Verse 30 clarifies this a little more:

> 30 *And any person that does any work in that same day, the same person will I destroy from among his people.*

We already know that our own works cannot save us or anyone else. We already know that our own works are not going to accomplish anything that is going to last forever. We already know that we need to rest in the Lord. If we rest in the Lord, he does his work in us and through us. In other words, he actually wants to use us to do something. This is by grace and through faith.

This is the controversy of the nonscriptural terminology of "death to self" and one of the reasons I believe we should return to scriptural terminology which speaks of denying our self (Luke 9:23) and of being *dead to sin* (Romans 6:2). There is some truth in death to self, but we must understand there is an old self and a new self. It is the old self that must die. The Scripture calls it the *old man*. And the old man is a slave to sin, but the new man is a servant to righteousness. The new man does righteousness – it just flows naturally out of him. It is a compulsive thing. The new man cannot stand to not do righteousness, while the old man only wants to sin. The new man in Christ is at rest, but the old man will never be at rest.

So friends, are you at rest?

Are you on fire?

God wants us to be the offering as we follow in the footsteps of Jesus. I always wonder: Did Abraham tell Sarah before he went out to offer up Isaac? I know that in my own life and ministry, there are certain things that we do not tell "Sarah." We just trust God that he is going to work things out in the end, as we believe him and follow his guidance step by step.

> 30 *And any person that does any work in that same day, the same person will I destroy from among his people.*

What day?

The day of the Lord prophesied by all the prophets.

> 31 *Ye shall do no manner of work; it shall be a perpetual statute throughout your ages in all your dwellings.*

This Day of Atonement, the Day of Reconciliation, the day when the people of God return to him will mark a huge change. As this time progresses, there will be no more "servile" work allowed for God's people. From this point on, it will all be his work, but we will be involved, tremendously involved.

God wants to give us the desires of our heart, but first he wants to purify our hearts and make sure that his heart is in us.

When that is the case, there will be no more problems. At that time, he will give us the desires of our heart because we will have his desires. The realm of the Holy of Holies is the realm of unlimited answered prayer (John 16:23).

Jesus did not suffer and die so we would not experience any trials or tribulation. He went to the cross to pay the penalty for our sins. He showed us the way and he is the way. He will carry us upon his shoulders into the Feast of Tabernacles, back into the realm of the presence of the Father, just as the names of all the tribes of Israel were engraved upon two onyx stones and set upon the shoulders of the ephod of the high priest (Exodus 28:6-14). We are to be joint heirs, sons, part of a many-membered body of Christ of which Jesus, our High Priest, is the Head.

> 32 *It shall be unto you a sabbath of sabbaths, and ye shall afflict your souls, beginning in the ninth day of the month in the evening, from evening unto evening, shall ye rest on your sabbath.*

Israel rested every seventh day under the law. Now we are entering into the seventh millennium from the creation of Adam. This is called the day of the Lord. For unto him one day is as a thousand years and a thousand years are as a day. Now we are to rest in him every day; we are to desist from our own works and allow him to work in and through us. Then he will light us on fire with his fire. Then all the promises will suddenly become "yes" and "amen" in fullness (2 Corinthians 1:20).

Note that the six thousand years (six prophetic days) of the government of man (which Adam forfeited to Satan) did not begin with the creation of Adam and Eve. They began when this "world" was founded – when Satan engineered the fall and Adam rebelled. So even though it is clear we have entered the seventh millennium (since the creation of Adam) and that the feast of trumpets is now upon us, the day of the Lord has not yet fully dawned.

First, the morning star must arise in our hearts as the fullness of the new day slowly dawns. This is the story of Esther.

Leviticus 23 continues on and describes the Feast of Tabernacles, which is typed with the age of the kingdom (Revelation 20). This was supposed to be the opening scene in the book of Esther, but Queen Vashti refused to enter in.

It would be tragic for any of us to have come all this way and to be cut off from reigning and ruling with Christ in the kingdom age because we did not repent and afflict our soul and desist from our own works at this most crucial and critical threshold.

Let us pray:

> *Heavenly Father, we ask that you might reveal yourself as never before, that we might seek you with all of our heart, that you might bring us to repentance in any area that is necessary, individually and corporately. Lord, we ask that we might see these things from your point of view and be able to understand the terrible damage that happens when we put our hand to that which only you can do. But on the other hand, we ask that we might have faith and that we might be encouraged to allow you to do your work in and through us.*
>
> *We ask that we may not shy away from anything you truly want us to do. We ask this in the name of the Lord Jesus Christ. Amen.*

About the Author

Russell Stendal, a former hostage of Colombian rebels, is a lifelong missionary to that same group in the jungles of Colombia. He is an influential friend to military and government leaders in Colombia, Cuba, Mexico, Venezuela, and the United States. Russell's ministry shares the gospel via twelve radio stations, hundreds of thousands of Bibles, books, and movies distributed through airplane parachute drops, and numerous speaking engagements for groups of leaders, prisoners, and individuals. Russell goes wherever the Lord leads, whether it's to speak with a president or to go deep into the jungle to help an individual in trouble. He has witnessed thousands commit their lives to Christ.

Connect with the Author

Website: www.cpcsociety.ca

Newsletter Signup: www.anekopress.com/stendal-newsletter

Russell and his coworkers have built dozens of radio stations in Latin America that concentrate a clear message on remote and dangerous areas where persecution of Christians is rampant. More than 120,000 Galcom solar-powered radios have been deployed to those being discipled. Most of the programming is in Spanish, but they also transmit in almost a dozen native languages where a great move of God is presently taking place. Russell  preaches through the Bible, a chapter or so per message. More than 1,000 messages have been recorded and aired repeatedly. The chapters of this book are samples of these messages preached on the radio in the Colombian war zone about ten years ago. The key website is www.fuerzadepaz.com. Pray for Russell and his team as they expand Spanish-language radio coverage into places like Cuba, Venezuela, Mexico, and Central America.

Plans are in the works for new stations broadcasting in English that will provide coverage into Africa (where there are over 300 million English speakers) and possibly even into Asia and the Middle East. The first stage, as the programming is refined, will be Internet radio. After that, we want to begin shortwave radio transmission and distribution of Galcom radios in Africa and elsewhere as God opens the doors. The new radios have digital audio Bibles on board, and the goal is to move in the direction of digital shortwave transmissions within the next few years.

Connect with Russell's Ministry

Website
www.cpcsociety.ca

Receive newsletter updates
http://goo.gl/amBsCD

Buy books
http://amzn.to/1nPLcNL

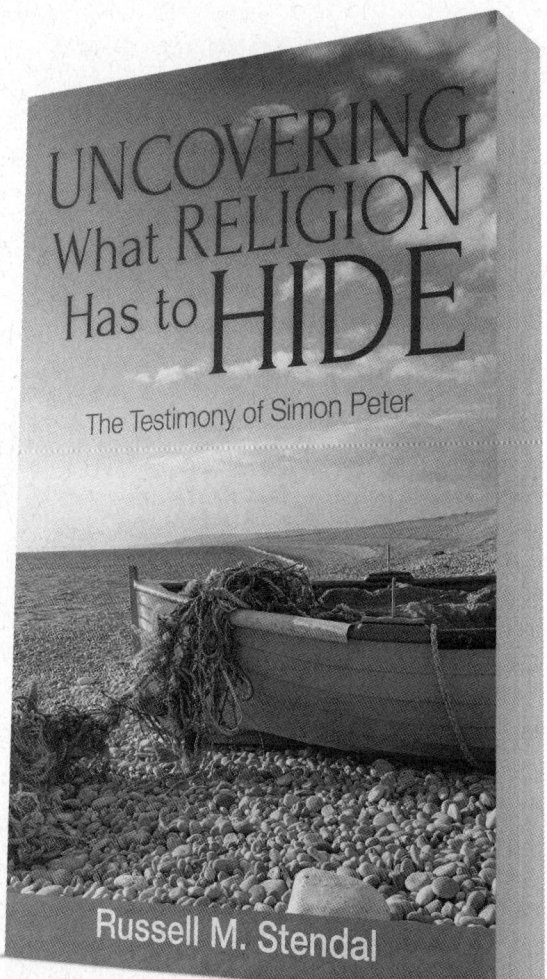

Peter made all the classical, Christian mistakes. He spoke before thinking, lacked faith, and even denied the Lord Jesus Christ. But Peter had a moldable, open heart, and the Lord knew it. All the mistakes Peter made helped him understand what other Christians face, and his writings both warn and encourage readers today.

Too many of today's religious entities and Christian individuals are functioning on spiritual autopilot, rarely pausing to pray in earnest and seek the Lord's will for their lives. Peter says if we lack the things of the Lord, we are blind and walk by feeling the way with our hands (2 Peter 1:9). His writings serve as an eye-opener for those who want to live for the Lord completely and without reservation.

Available where books are sold